C.S. LEWIS
ON LITERATURE

An Introduction to His
Literary Criticism
Literary History
Literary Theory

MARCUS K. PAUL

ADVANCE PRAISE

Marcus Paul's *C. S. Lewis on Literature* is an excellent introduction to the major professional writing of Lewis's career, namely his works of literary criticism, history, and theory. This book will help anyone trying to comprehend the interconnectedness of Lewis's literary output. As Owen Barfield once said about Lewis: 'somehow what he thought about everything was secretly present in what he said about anything.' Paul has done his work well - he makes me want to re-read Lewis - and the questions for further study at the end of this work make it suitable for use in the classroom or even a book club.

Will Vaus, Pastor of First Congregational Church, Yarmouth, MA. Author of 17 books, including *C. S. Lewis's Top Ten: Influential Books & Authors* and *The Hidden Story of Narnia*.

Marcus Paul's introduction to C. S. Lewis's scholarly writings on literature reveals not only their astonishing scope, profound intelligence and learning, but also their accessibility to the non-specialist. Paul's arrangement of the material, working back from the twentieth century to the sixteenth, accords with Lewis's sense of historical depth, perceptible in the contemporary for those whose eyes have been helped to see it. But Paul's greatest achievement in this guide is in having seen the absolute integrity – in both senses – of Lewis's work: all, whether academic, apologist, or "creative", as we now call it (Lewis would surely have disliked the term), was one in a life lived in faith.

Jean Ward, Professor of Literature in English at the Institute of English and American Studies, University of Gdańsk, Poland Author of *The Between-Space of Translation: Literary Sketches*

Marcus Paul's welcome new study illuminates an aspect of Lewis's achievement often strangely neglected. Here we see the fruits Lewis's work in his day job, that of a literary scholar and teacher of literature.

John V Fleming, Louis W Fairchild Professor of English and Comparative Literature Emeritus at Princeton University

ADVANCE PRAISE

Lewis's output as a literary historian, critic and theorist was astonishingly large. The number of scholars who have paid serious and sustained attention to it is astonishingly small. But these lines of work constituted his professional career as a distinguished academic first at Oxford and latterly at Cambridge and deserve to receive much more careful consideration. Marcus Paul is to be commended for this helpful and well-written survey and for highlighting Lewis's key advice to all literary people, namely that we should read to enlarge and liberate the self, not just entertain it or confirm its preconceptions. Useful, thorough, thoughtful.

> Michael Ward, University of Oxford
> Co-editor of *The Cambridge Companion to C. S. Lewis*

Marcus Paul's *C. S. Lewis on Literature* finally addresses a yawning gap in Lewis scholarship, that is, Lewis's own scholarship. Though others have commented on the master's literary theory and criticism, none has done so as systematically, thoroughly, and engagingly. This pioneering work is quite possibly a landmark that will show others the way further in. It certainly taught me much.

> James Como, Professor Emeritus of Rhetoric, York College (CUNY)
> Author (most recently) of *C. S. Lewis: A Very Short Introduction* (Oxford) and *Mystical Perelandra* (Winged Lion Press).

In *C. S. Lewis on Literature,* readers of Lewis's fiction, theology, and apologetics will discover the delightful instruction found in his 'professional works'.

> David Llewellyn Dodds
> Editor of *Arthurian Poets: Charles Williams* (Arthurian Studies, 24) Former Lecturer of English at Harlaxton College and former Curator of C.S. Lewis's house, The Kilns.

C. S. Lewis on Literature

An Introduction to His
Literary Criticism – Literary History – Literary Theory

Copyright © 2024 Marcus Paul

Winged Lion Press
Hamden, CT

All rights reserved. Except in the case of quotations embodied in critical articles or reviews, no part of this book may be reproduced or transmitted in any form or by any means, electronic or mechanical, including photocopying, recording, or by any storage system.

Winged Lion Press

ISBN 978-1-935688-55-6

for Elaine

CONTENTS

INTRODUCTION   1

PART ONE
Literary Criticism
from the 20th to 16th century

CHAPTER ONE: 11
J. R. R. Tolkien, Charles Williams, George Orwell, Dorothy Sayers, Rudyard Kipling, and Rider Haggard:
fairy stories, myth, the Inner Ring, the gospel of work

CHAPTER TWO: 21
William Morris, Sir Walter Scott and Jane Austen:
longing and meaning, facing reality, overvaluing art and artist, putting second things first, undeceptions, ethics, plots and making sense of the world

CHAPTER THREE: 33
Joseph Addison, John Bunyan and The Bible:
Rational Piety v. faith, Romanticism and art, how allegory and parables work, narrowness of view, translating the Bible, its future

CHAPTER FOUR: 45
John Milton: *A Preface to Paradise Lost:*
how to read the poem, the first principle of criticism, the nature of epic, the grand style, the depiction and dissection of Satan, insights to human nature, a bold conclusion

CHAPTER FIVE: 55
John Donne and William Shakespeare:
taste and 'chronological snobbery', the need to be on guard, terms 'Puritan' and 'Catholic' misconceived, importance of universal criteria, Shakespeare's unique genius, how to read and listen to his plays, seeing 'character' through plot and poetry, a new view of *Hamlet*

PART TWO
LITERARY HISTORY

FROM THE CLASSICAL PERIOD TO THE 16TH CENTURY

CHAPTER SIX: 71
"On Reading Old Books" and *The Allegory of Love*:
old books as a corrective to present error, polytheism and monotheism, duty and desire, introspection and allegory, dying and rising – a law of life, Plato and Narnia, *The Faerie Queene* and theological truth

CHAPTER SEVEN: 87
"The Genesis of a Medieval Book", *The Discarded Image* **and "Imagination and Thought in the Middle Ages"**:
necessity of critiquing the book not the author, the Medieval Model of the universe the supreme creation of the time, Earth – the intellectual and spiritual 'edge' of the cosmos, our own Model created as much by our psychology as by facts

CHAPTER EIGHT: 99
English Literature in the Sixteenth Century:
the Middle Ages and Renaissance not two distinct periods, the background to the period, misconceiving the past (e.g. magic and astrology,) Humanists and Puritans, voyages of discovery, Christians' views of Empire, the nature of 'Man', the role of Tyndale as theologian and translator, the literary value of the Authorised Version

PART THREE
LITERARY THEORY

CHAPTER NINE:
"Christianity and Literature", "High and Low Brows"   117
and *The Personal Heresy*:
creativity or imitation?, not valuing literature for its own sake, art as a religion, literary snobbery, 'Style', taste and fashion, humility and avoiding vanity, focus on the poem not the poet, looking through the window not at it, 'poetolatry'

CHAPTER TEN:
Studies in Words and *An Experiment in Criticism*:   133
the best language, 'verbicide', insulation via context, 'tactical definitions', emotional language, how to write well, profanity and abuse, writing criticism, avoiding self-indulgence, 'using' and 'receiving' literature, myth, escapism, fairy-stories and 'childish' appetites, entertainment, criticism in schools, why do we read?, leave the self behind, a concluding epiphany

POSTSCRIPT	151
APPENDIX	
C. S. Lewis on Children's Literature	157
POINTS & QUESTIONS FOR FURTHER STUDY	167
INDEX	179
LIST OF LEWIS'S NON-FICTION CITED	187
ACKNOWLEDGEMENTS	189
BOOKS FROM WINGED LION PRESS	193

INTRODUCTION

C. S. Lewis began his teaching career one hundred years ago in 1924 at University College Oxford, moving to Magdalen College in 1925. He taught in small lecture rooms and gave one-to-one tutorials. Today, through his writing, millions of Christians continue to be taught by him. But how many access his literary scholarship and lectures? A storehouse of unexplored treasures lies in wait for those who want them. This book opens the door to twelve of Lewis's books of literary history, criticism and theory – and invites us in.

C. S. Lewis loved stories. He grew up living in the imaginative worlds their authors created. From the earliest age he was writing his own stories, creating his own worlds – stories of Boxen, its people, its rulers, its animals. At school and under William Kirkpatrick, his tutor prior to entering Oxford, he read fiction voraciously alongside his daily study of classical authors in preparation for reading 'Mods and Greats' at the University. Despite his 'double first' in this, he decided, as is well known, to read for an English Literature degree and achieved another 'first' after a single year rather than three – at least in part because he had already read so much of the canon of this supreme literary heritage.

By the time he was appointed Professor at Cambridge he was widely considered to be one of the best-read men of his generation.[1] One reason for this was that he read not solely as a professional duty but because he loved to do it. For him, there was never a book long enough or a cup of tea big enough.[2] The linking of the two ideas

---

1 A N Wilson, *C. S. Lewis, A Biography* (Collins, 1990) p.161
2 C.S. Lewis, *Of Other Worlds: Essays and Stories,* Ed. Walter Hooper (Bles 1966) p. v

is revealing: he saw them both as homely, everyday, commonplace pleasures, but with an essential difference: reading a book properly will expand and enhance who you are. So reading good books well was, for him, something to encourage and teach everyone to do.

There is a real sense in which he spent the larger part of his life seeking to demonstrate this in his teaching work at both Oxford and Cambridge, and in every 'literary' book he penned for publication. His apologetic and devotional works, most of his readers will agree, are uniquely persuasive or moving or illuminating, but they are not the books which took him the longest to write. We know too that he was writing the Narnia stories in his 'spare time' while the larger academic books gradually took shape. His fiction – both for children and adults – did not require, in and of itself, the scholarly research and long library hours that went into *The Allegory of Love* or *English Literature in the Sixteenth Century*[3] or *Studies in Words*, to mention a few. Though serious in purpose, Lewis's excursions into popular theology for (as he would say) 'the man in the street' were almost a relief from pressure of work, in terms of effort a mere *bagatelle* in comparison with his major *opera*.

And yet, it is these superb, compelling, crystalline essays and Christian polemics that most people are familiar with today and not his books about books. Many readers of Lewis's apologetic and devotional works have never approached this treasury with its capacity to enrich our wider reading. They believe them, perhaps, to be irrelevant to their interests and concerns or too difficult or too technical for those unfamiliar with the texts and periods he describes. "Yet in the end", as Derek Brewer wrote, "the secular and

---

3 This took fifteen years to complete. See *The Cambridge Companion to C. S. Lewis*, Ed. R MacSwain and M Ward (Cambridge University Press, 2010) p.23

HIS LITERARY CRITICISM, HISTORY, THEORY

religious writings, however various and controversial, are part of the same eager sympathetic imagination."[4] And both John Lawlor and J. A. W. Bennett remarked that his works are "all of a piece" and that there was no split in his personality: the visionary and the moralist, in him, were at one.[5]

It may be a surprise for such readers to find that such imaginative unity is the case. But the discovery to be made is that Lewis's academic writing is often illuminating for the ordinary or non-specialist reader in the same way as his writing on 'religion' has often proved compelling for those who normally steer clear of such topics. Indeed, countless readers owe their first interest in Christianity to something that they read in Lewis.

Nevertheless, we must ask, are the academic books somehow less important? If we agree that the saving of a single soul is more important than all the art and literature of the world, then, yes, they are.[6] Does that mean that they are deserving of neglect by Christians who are not literary specialists? I do not believe so. As Prof. J.V. Fleming of Princeton University wrote: "I would argue that his literary scholarship is, from the point of view of writing skill alone, his greatest work".[7]

I begin with the assumption that all Lewis fans are inevitably, to some extent, readers. They will have read at least one or two of

---

4 Harry Lee Poe & Rebecca Whitten Poe (Eds.) *C. S. Lewis Remembered*, (Zondervan, 2006) p.71

5 Jocelyn Gibb (Ed.), *Light on Lewis*, (Geoffrey Bles, 1965) pp. 49,80,82.

6 Lewis wrote that the Christian knows from the start that the salvation of a single soul is more important than the writing and studying of all the epics and tragedies ever penned. *Christian Reflections* (Bles, 1967) p. 10

7 In *The Cambridge Companion*, p.27.

his books of apologetics (*Mere Christianity* or *The Screwtape Letters*). In all likelihood they will have read the Narnia stories, perhaps the science fiction too. Both the subject-matter and the style of all those books are determined in part by Lewis's own reading – of history, of fiction, of theology. Reading, then, is something we all share a common enjoyment in and would like to get better at: in order to understand more deeply, feel more sensitively, to deduce or anticipate ideas more quickly and accurately.

Next, we need to ask, what it is which has prevented so many readers of his other works from opening his books of literary history and criticism. The obvious answer is that they were written originally for the specialist reader, one engaged in literary studies, at one level or another, and that their focus on the literature of a past age would not seem to be relevant to present day needs, concerns and faith. I would want to argue that that is a wrong approach. We should not be starting with the idea of relevance but with an idea of the relative *importance* of different aspects of Christian living. How important is it, for those of us blessed with reading capabilities, to recognise, to understand, to contextualise today's attitudes, thinking and their consequent events within the 'conversation' of the literature of the western world down through the ages? In a word, to be equipped intellectually to live as thinking Christians in the twenty-first century? If Lewis was right in his lecture, "De Descriptione Temporum" [8], that we are more cut off today from the past than previous ages have ever been (and, incidentally, that Christians have a standing advantage over others in understanding the past) then the matter is very important in our need to preserve a historic faith while living in a chaotic, pluralistic, syncretistic

---

8   His 1955 inaugural lecture at Cambridge: "Christians and Pagans had much more in common with each than either has with a post-Christian".

and ever more rapidly changing world. A knowledge of what has been said and thought already – by poets and philosophers, by playwrights and novelists – helps us to see current thinking as part of a process, no more authoritative by being 'modern' than any previously 'modern' period.

One of Lewis's most particular gifts as a critic was to make his writing such that his readers could enjoy all that he was telling them without their having read the texts he refers to. "In his chosen fields", Professor Nevill Coghill wrote, "he was easily the greatest teacher of our time" whose major books of history and criticism represent an unequalled achievement in his day.[9] The drama critic, Kenneth Tynan, one of Lewis's more famous pupils, found Lewis as a teacher "incomparable" and "immensely invigorating, stimulating and inspiring".[10] Walter Hooper, his secretary, once said that Lewis sounded like his books[11] and Nevil Coghill that his essays were filled with "comparisons and contrasts that sparkled and exploded in his conversation".[12] Lewis, as critic, wrote also as a practising poet and novelist combining his skills in those fields with his erudite scholarship and his powers of philosophical analysis.

This was more than just a matter of finding the apposite analogy, quotation, or even of cleverly evoking the context and spirit of the writing – though Lewis does all this. It is also that he brings about "a respectful introduction between a reader and his work"[13], giving us the privilege, as it were, of allowing us to meet these famous and brilliant people and converse with them in a way

---

9 Poe Op. Cit. p. 65
10 *The C.S. Lewis Encyclopedia*, Colin Duriez (Azure books, 2002) p. 215
11 Ibid. p.50
12 Gibb, Op. Cit. p.54
13 Fleming in *The Cambridge Companion* p.19

that otherwise time, space and our own hesitance would preclude.

But frequently it is also because he invites his reader to join him in the just cause he is defending. Lewis was almost never a non-combatant. For him, George Watson noted, "Intellectual fashion existed only in order to be tested and refuted".[14] Truth, he felt, in every sphere was always vulnerable and prevailing attitudes easily mistaken or founded on false principles which could be exposed by clear logical thinking. This sheds light on his famous Socratic Society appearances at Oxford. They were not simply performances in apologetics, but rather a symptom of the way his mind worked. As Paul Piehler, another of Lewis's tutees wrote: "[H]is scholarly and religious lives were really no more separable than two sides of the same coin."[15] In matters of importance there were, for Lewis, right and wrong ways of looking at things and the evidence available to support the right should, he believed, be used in an adversarial manner so as not to let falsehood flourish or become the dangerous basis for further untruths in any field of study. Literature is the expression of a mind which points to something other than itself.[16] If what is pointed at is important, revealing, delightful, an insight to a past age, then there is a responsibility to understand that as well as we can. Watching others misconstrue a text and doing nothing about the error struck Lewis as profoundly wrong. If we add to this that it was sometimes Christian writers who were misconstrued to their detriment then the stakes were raised even higher.

He realised, and on one occasion stated, that in the final analysis, the ground of a disagreement was often metaphysical

---

14 Poe, Op. Cit. p. 86
15 Ibid. p.126
16 Lewis especially liked this aspect of medieval poetry. The poets of the day did not receive fame but gave it. See *English Literature in the Sixteenth Century*, (Oxford University Press 1954) p.27

rather than literary. Others' dislike of his assertion that many critics did not like Milton's depiction of God in *Paradise Lost* because they simply did not like God (see Ch.XIX of *A Preface To Paradise Lost*), was probably because it was so near the mark – a metaphysical, not literary divide.

Lewis was especially gifted in writing about the periods he made his main focus. His ability to imagine himself back into the period in a deeply informed way, his easy familiarity with all the languages in his source materials and his far-reaching insights into human nature enable him to take his readers into realms they had not dreamed of nor, perhaps, even knew existed. The testimony both of academics and a wider readership is that he could 're-animate the past'[17] with his 'unique combination of different types of learning' as no other could. In the poets especially, he found a vision of the world suffused with the knowledge of a good and loving Creator which reinforced his own.

If we accept both the importance of what Lewis was doing in his academic writing, and its brilliance of style and conception, the next logical step would be to explore the territory – its breath-taking grandeur and sweeping views as well as its individual gemstones and beauty spots. We need therefore a map to guide us through this (to many) largely unexplored country.

Broadly speaking, the territory can be divided into three areas:

1. Literary criticism on writers dating from his own contemporaries back to the sixteenth century.
2. The writings on literary history from classical times to the sixteenth century.
3. Essays and books on literary theory.

---

17   Jocelyn Gibb, Op. Cit. p. xi, p. 47

In each of these areas of the map we will be able to locate features of unique value to readers today, or, to continue the metaphor, to find buried treasure worth many times the effort of traversing the landscape. We will begin with a look at some of Lewis's writing about the twentieth and nineteenth centuries.

PART ONE

LITERARY CRITICISM FROM THE 20TH TO 16TH CENTURY

CHAPTER ONE

FAIRY STORIES, ESCAPISM AND MYTH

We begin with the modern period because it is the easiest to access and many names will be familiar to those who have an interest in books: Lewis's friends, J. R. R. Tolkien and Dorothy Sayers; the dystopian writer George Orwell of *Animal Farm* fame; Rudyard Kipling and Rider Haggard – writers of exotic, if Imperial, adventure stories.

Here, as everywhere, Lewis is inclined to praise the writing and authors, not just from generosity of spirit but because he believed a critic writes better and more instructively when writing about books we like.[1]

It is often imagined that Lewis wrote exclusively about previous ages but he was an acute reader and critic of his contemporaries. In writing about the books of his friend, **J. R. R. Tolkien**, (*The Hobbit* and *Lord of the Rings)* he touches on the topics of Romanticism, myth, how to write for children, the abnormality of much contemporary writing, as well as humanity's unchanging predicament and clues to a solution. His view was that a good children's book could be read ten or twenty times by adults because they would increasingly realise what 'profound reflection' had gone into it – just as it had into *Lord of the Rings*, a book, he wrote, containing "beauties which pierce like swords or burn like cold iron." Lewis sees the book as having the status of myth because it is so widely applicable to each reader, a sort of master key to every lock, to every realm we live in. Allegory, by contrast, points to a specific political or psychological situation.

---

1 See Lewis's *An Experiment in Criticism* (Cambridge University Press, 1961) esp. Chap. XI

Lewis was also concerned to answer the charge that such 'fantasy' writing was escapist. As so often in his apologetics he turns the charge on its head. What we escape from, he wrote, is the illusions of everyday life, from the prevailing but mistaken idea that there is nothing heroic or wonderful about most experience. Individuals, perhaps even our species, pitted against the universe is our unchanging predicament – which heroic ages recognised better than us. Until, he suggests, we have seen ourselves as heroes in a fairy-tale we have not really seen ourselves at all. There is "good cheer" but there is also anguish in such stories, though it is an anguish that we know can be lifted, and *once* had not been there at all.

Christians will have picked up the theological echoes and understanding in each of these points, but there is more. Lewis also distils from Tolkien the idea that our fate so often depends on the smallest thing, on the seemingly weakest character or on an overlooked event. Lewis sees this as a supreme structural device: it goes to the heart of reality and adds not only to the grandeur but also the pathos of the story. It gives us fresh eyes on our own existence. Neither an easy optimism nor a 'wailing pessimism' is adequate, only an awareness that every victory is impermanent and has to be jealously guarded. Our battle against evil is ongoing.

Thus we can see that this essay on Tolkien (in fact a review) is a particularly fine example of how Lewis manages to use a single text to open windows into other and larger worlds and more fully to understand our own. However, to understand adequately his usage of the idea of Romance in the review we would need to read his Preface to *The Pilgrim's Regress*. Nevertheless, we can see straightaway that his definition of myth is a profound one – myth is not merely a legend or child's story but a 'master key'. Tantalisingly

HIS LITERARY CRITICISM, HISTORY, THEORY

there is a hint here of an idea that lies at the back of almost all Lewis wrote; he suggests that the facility to make a genuine myth ('mythopoeia') is not a matter of subjective creativity but of insight into a deeper reality that mostly eludes us.

Lewis explains that by putting bread or gold or apples (or other archetypes) into a myth, we do not make reality more distant but rediscover it. The same is true he says of good and evil, of our anguish, our perils and our joy. Good and evil are not just names for the things we like and dislike, as some would have us believe, but are the polarities between which we live and act out this drama of life. People's real lives have a heroic and mythical quality. Myth is a sort of mirror – and when we look at a landscape in a mirror we seem to see it for the first time. He will have a good deal more to teach us about this in his much later book, *An Experiment in Criticism*.[2]

Seeing things in a new way is also the central thrust of Lewis's appreciation of **Charles Williams**' novels. In a BBC broadcast of 1949 he explores not so much the difference between realistic or "straight" fiction and fantasy writing in which a "frontier" is violated, but rather a more subtle distinction. He is concerned to show that Williams, like E. Nesbit, F. Anstey, *Alice* and *Gulliver* with their everyday, matter-of-fact characters, creates not an allegory but an experiment with ideas. But Williams, unlike some others, creates an 'invaded' world, not just to turn the spotlight on the follies and oddities of our own world but also on the far side of the frontier, a very different world. The two passages Lewis singles out as being most powerfully illuminating are both about death. It is a topic that he found of much interest – as we shall see when we come to his views on *Hamlet*. The depiction of an

---

2 This will be dealt with in the section on Literary Theory.

'invaded' world suffuses, of course, all of Lewis's own fiction and *That Hideous Strength* most nearly approximates to Williams' use of an 'ordinary' academic setting for its plot.

When it comes to the work of **George Orwell**, we can see myth of a very different kind from Tolkien's. It is immediately apparent that Lewis thinks *Animal Farm* a far greater book than *1984* which he sees as too indulgent, too full of the author's own predispositions and concerns and insufficiently 'pruned' to be a major work of art. *Animal Farm* is distanced from Orwell's personality into becoming myth and, paradoxically, uses animals to make the characters more revealingly human: a mix of good, bad, pitiable and honourable. Lewis wrote the piece in 1955 when he was still engaged in writing his own Narnia stories about talking animals who are highly recognisable as human types and individuals. The creatures in the stories strongly convey ideas of good and evil but Lewis manages this without seeming to preach – something he praised in one of his contemporaries, Dorothy Sayers.

EVANGELISM AND ART

Lewis's generous tribute to **Dorothy Sayers** – scholar, poet and detective story writer – gives occasion for an opinion on the topic of how creative art and preaching mix. Sayers was much admired by Lewis; she was forthright as a Christian apologist and her combative stance, along with her deep understanding of the Medieval world meant that she shared much in common with him. However, in his 1958 'panegyric' for her he makes clear that she was right never to allow the evangelist to take over when she was acting as an artist and entertainer. If she had done so, they both agreed, not only would the theology be bad, but so would the art. When writing of Milton, Lewis noted that the conception of poetry that the great poet held precluded him drawing attention to his own idiosyncratic views and instead putting first whatever would delight and instruct his readers. *Paradise Lost* is not specifically Protestant but adopts a theology that is catholic – shared by Christians everywhere at all times.[3] Lewis's own theology aimed at the same[4] and his stories, he often reminded people, were not covert attempts to convert readers but visions of a different reality, explorations of ideas.[5] It is something that some practitioners today should ponder.

THE GOSPEL OF WORK AND THE INNER RING

"The Inner Ring" will be a concept familiar to many readers of Lewis's ethical and theological essays (and some of his fiction) but not all will know that he wrote a brilliant analysis of the work of **Rudyard Kipling** (1865-1936) in which this idea is central. Journalist, poet, novelist and short story writer, he has long been a figure of controversy. Writers such as T. S. Eliot and George Orwell had sharply contrasting views about his work while acknowledging a certain greatness or genius about him. Both his stories for adults and his children's books remain in print and have given rise to films (e.g. Disney's 2016, *The Jungle Book*), TV documentaries, cartoons and music.

Lewis's interest in bringing wider issues before his audience rather than merely, strictly speaking, the text itself – without reference to its relevance to our everyday world – becomes very apparent towards the end of his long essay called "Kipling's World." In it, one of his central points is that Kipling is "the poet of work". The phrase seems unremarkable but in fact is the reverse; poets

---

3 *A Preface to Paradise Lost* (Oxford University Press, 1942) p.90
4 See his *Preface* to *Mere Christianity* (Geoffrey Bless, 1952)
5 Rowan Williams, *The Lion's World* (SPCK, 2012) p. 4

before Kipling had avoided the topic – and yet it is our daily work which occupies most of our time and energy. Crime, sport, love affairs, ill-luck in poetry, yes, but work, no. Of itself, this seems to be merely an interesting literary observation but characteristically, Lewis turns it into an acute insight to human behaviour as deeply illuminating to the general reader as to the academic: he helps us see ourselves. As the English diarist, Samuel Pepys (1633-1703) noted, men get great pleasure talking about their work. Some of our strongest emotions derive from it, especially when that work is shared or of the same kind. In our own day, it has often been remarked, men make friendships more by doing things together than by merely talking; women often more easily achieve friendship *only* by talking.

What Lewis reveals so tellingly about Kipling's writing and about ourselves is the impact that this "ruthless monster" of work has on us – for better or worse. The impression which Kipling's stories leave us with is that work forces us to conform to its demands; we have to "be licked into shape" before we are useful. One reason, we are then told, why people dislike Kipling is that this depiction of humanity as being a creature that needs quite severe treatment before we are useful for anything, has affinities with the doctrine of original sin – a teaching which is even more controversial today than in the last century. Another reason for some to dislike Kipling's stories, is that this process may well involve what we would see as bullying, even cruelty, in the workplace. In our society that behaviour is now rightly unacceptable but the corollary of disallowing this has been a growing industry of defending 'Human Rights'. Lewis then points out that by treating employees unjustly we force them to be preoccupied with their rights rather than learning their trade (he suggests climbing a mast, cleaning a sewer or joining an army) which, if widespread, would

HIS LITERARY CRITICISM, HISTORY, THEORY

endanger or impoverish us all.

This naturally leads Lewis to reflect on how work relationships can often develop – and so he approaches the topic of 'the Inner Ring'. It was one borne out by his own experience and appears in his literary criticism, ethical/theological writing and his fiction. Thus, while still writing about Kipling he opens up his most far-reaching reflections on the subtle temptations and pitfalls of our daily work patterns. He shows that while Kipling rebukes the exploiting employer there is, even so, something deeply unsatisfying about his depiction. To prove the pointedness of the rebuke, Lewis quotes Kipling's lines:

> When the last grim joke is entered
> In the big black Book of Jobs
> And Quetta graveyards give again
> Their victims to the air,
> I shouldn't like to be the man
> Who sent Jack Barret there.

But irrespective of the suffering of the labourer, for Kipling, the work must go on – in armies, hospitals, building, administering Empire. Protest against terms of service, he might say, will not bring the ship into harbour. Such a doctrine, claims Lewis, conceals a terrible void or lack of point at its heart. It is a gospel of work, of progress: all blind and naked and uncritical of itself. None of the questions about the ultimate purpose or beneficence of it all are ever raised.

The reason the purpose is not ever questioned is because of the open but unspoken secret at the heart of the process: the intimacy of the closed circle, the Inner Ring. It is the brotherhood of a shared profession which can take priority over the work itself.

When it does, to be within the circle becomes a status that must be maintained even if "cruelty, extortion, oppression and dishonesty" are the cost. For those of us in work, or even in any social groupings, there is a stark warning here of the ease with which this temptation can overtake us: "the exquisite pleasure of being approved". This aspect of our lives in the workplace is depicted with convincing authenticity in Chapter Two of *That Hideous Strength* and the concept makes its way into *The Dark Tower, Perelandra* and *The Great Divorce* as well as being the topic for his 1944 Memorial Oration at King's College, London. But Lewis found it first, and most fully developed, in Kipling. Whether he knew that Kipling was himself a 'mason', that is, he belonged to the (then) secretive Order of Freemasons for the whole of his adult life and rose to be a Master Mason – an 'inner' member of an Inner Ring – we cannot be sure.

Ironically, having depicted the 'Inner Ring' so powerfully and uncritically, Kipling himself was later the victim of literary coteries minded to dismiss him from any inner circle of revered authors. Lewis, by contrast, despite these reservations, accorded him merit of a very high order.

A NOTE ON 'CHARACTER' AND MYTH

The Victorian novelist, **Rider Haggard** (1856 – 1925), (*King Solomon's Mines, She*) is not someone much read today but his legacy lives on through his influence on Kipling, Conan Doyle's *Sherlock Holmes* stories and the Indiana Jones films. Lewis loved the stories simply as stories because they were examples of the "mythopoeic gift pure and simple". He reminds us too that the absence of any detailed study of character in them is not a fault but is appropriate for the adventure story genre. To be trusty, treacherous or cowardly overrides the need for 'character' which is the luxury of those who live beyond basic necessity and out of danger. It's a useful insight when considering Lewis's own 'adventure' stories – whether in Narnia or his science-fiction.[6]

---

[6] Lewis's criticism on Tolkien, Williams, Orwell, Sayers and Haggard may be found in C. S. Lewis, *C. S. Lewis on Stories and Other Essays on Literature,* Ed. Walter Hooper (Harcourt Brace Jovanovich 1982), ed. W Hooper. That on Kipling in "Kipling's World" in *Selected Literary Essays* (1969) ed. W Hooper. *They Asked for a Paper* (1962) contains Lewis's 'oration' on "The Inner Ring"

CHAPTER TWO

LONGING AND MEANING: FACING REALITY

The mind of C. S. Lewis, as we have said, was highly integrated. Reality for him did not consist of dislocated parts which contained elements that contradicted each other. God's universe was self-consistent and the minds he gave us to interpret it were capable, despite appearances to the contrary, of making sense of it. Literature, for Lewis, besides being a delight and diversion, was also a means of understanding God's world better. A really good book, he believed, would cast some further light on the human predicament. Few writers could do this more powerfully than one whose books few today will have opened, or perhaps even heard of: **William Morris** (1834-1896).

Lewis's early essay on Morris is a fine example of his ability to invite his readers on to his 'side' and to take part in a debate even when we have not read 'the papers in the case'. In our day, Morris is best known for his textile designs and as a social activist within the British Arts and Crafts Movement. But he was also a poet, a novelist and an artist aligned with the Pre-Raphaelites. He was author of the epic poems, *The Earthly Paradise, The Life and Death of Jason,* and *Sigurd the Volsung* – the last of which was an influence on Tolkien.[1]

Insights about readers and reading come thick and fast in the essay. We will see that Lewis will defend the reputation of Pagan or non-Christian authors as much as Christian if they are great writers and have new things to show us. He judges Morris to be the most irreligious of all the poets and quite unaware of

---

1 See Humphrey Carpenter's *J.R.R. Tolkien: A Biography* (George Allen & Unwin, 1977) p.77

the 'Christian and sacramental' view of things but has the highest praise for him as a writer. In part, this is because he finds in *The Earthly Paradise* his familiar doctrine of 'longing'(*Sehnsucht*) which is the experience which drives us to search for meaning beyond the mundane and material. Written in 1937, this is one of his first academic explorations of the idea. For those who know the doctrine from his other works his expression of it here will add a new level of meaning.

Today, in the West, formal religion may be in decline, but religion has many disguises. Spiritual and 'moral' alternatives grow year on year. Astrology, the climate movement, conspiracy theories, avoidance of apocalypse, are but a few, and the completely secular movements can be as judgemental as old Calvinism could often be. There is a resurgent obsession with purity, with the public humiliation of heretics and the original sin of 'unconscious bias'. In Morris, Lewis sees someone who cuts through such surface obfuscation to the profounder truth behind such ephemeral movements, into the causes that give rise to them. 'Materialists' (unbelievers) tend to repress this truth whilst Christians explain it. Morris does neither but presents characters unable to stop themselves reaching out for meaning, for *something*, beyond our visible world. As such, he is the best possible objective witness to this telling aspect of our humanity. In his work an irresolvable tension arises between our impression of the goodness of mere living[2] and the sting of our mortality. It is not unhappiness which gives rise to misgivings about ultimate meaning, but (perhaps unexpectedly) happiness which poignantly reminds us of its own, and our, transience. As Byron realised, it is pleasure that is the

---

2 Orual experiences this despite her dangerous mission in *Till We Have Faces*. See p.104

HIS LITERARY CRITICISM, HISTORY, THEORY

sternest moralist.[3] If you want to know more about *longing*, Lewis is effectively saying, read William Morris.

In Morris, our mortality therefore is balanced (in *The Life and Death of Jason*) by 'the haunting desire for immortality'. His Argonauts, confronted with paradisal gardens and islands, find doleful thoughts pressing in on them; find too that the antidote is to get on with the task in hand – mending or gathering or sailing.[4] This is a curiously twenty-first century piece of therapy; but there is more to learn. Morris reminds us that his characters live in a world made (by the gods), not for happiness but to be 'a tale' – one in which we are all involved. At that point, Lewis tells us, Morris gets cold feet as he realises this almost leads to a reason

> "Why the brave man's spear is broken, and his war-shield fails at need."

But this is altogether too quasi-theological for the poet and he does not want that sort of simplification.[5]

What Lewis has placed his unerring finger on here is the perennial avoidance that each post-Enlightenment age has demonstrated. As thoughtful readers begin to follow through the implications both of experience and logic, there is, so often, an

---

[3] It is remarkable that a writer as different from Morris as Albert Camus wrote: "Beauty is unbearable, drives us to despair, offering us for a minute the glimpse of an eternity that we should like to stretch out over the whole of time." (Notebooks 1941-52). In *Till We Have Faces* Lewis would make Psyche tell Orual that it was when she was happiest that she "longed most". (p.82)

[4] In *Till We Have Faces*, the narrator, Orual, tells us that "sweat" is a much better cure than philosophy for "ill thoughts". (p.99)

[5] Something very similar happens to Orual in writing her "complaint" against the gods in *Till We Have Faces*. She tells us the gods used her pen to examine her own wounds (p.263). Her complaint turned out to be her answer. (p.305)

C.S. LEWIS ON LITERATURE

'Escape from Reason' as Francis Schaeffer termed it. T.S. Eliot's line, "Humankind cannot bear very much reality" applies to the atheist, we would want to say, more so than to the Christian.

Morris seems to have prefigured here some symptoms (and a cure) of the depressive illnesses which beset the twenty-first century in a way that the laborious back-breaking toil of so many Victorians made a rarity rather than endemic. (In 2023 a major study found that altruistic acts in particular were more effective than therapy in relieving depression[6]). But Morris, uncomfortable with reaching an almost theological position, retreated from it. This surely is not unlike what Lewis found pressing in on himself, but did not retreat from, thus becoming 'the most reluctant convert in all England'. Nevertheless, Lewis saw that Morris had value which both the 'militant Christians' and the determined materialists could benefit from. Christians will see an unrivalled clarity in his statement of the dilemma which all religions claim to address: the conflict between our natural desires to serve ourselves and the call of virtue to serve others. Lewis realised that all philosophical religion starts at this point. Materialists, on the other hand, will support Morris's vision that it is our duty to promote human happiness – even though this can only be fleeting according to their philosophy, in a species on a planet doomed to extinction.

Lewis's conclusion to this revealing essay is that neither optimism nor pessimism is adequate; they are "philosophies of the nursery". Our experience demands a creed which embraces both sweetness and melancholy and which shows how the one passes into the other and why. *Because* Morris faces such fundamental facts, although there are greater writers than he, none, Lewis tells us, are more profound in this respect.

---

[6] 'Being kind beats therapy for depression' (*The Times*, 12/1/23)

HIS LITERARY CRITICISM, HISTORY, THEORY

There is much in this early piece that anticipates both Lewis's apologetics (e.g. *The Problem of Pain*), and also his fiction, especially the Narnia stories and *Till We Have Faces*. There are parallels to be drawn in the thinking and shared images of the three disparate genres – his criticism, his apologetics and his fiction. It is a further demonstration of the essential integrity of his work: it is all a unity.

NOT OVERVALUING ART

One theme that runs through Lewis's academic writing from start to finish is his belief (and of course his argument) that we should not overvalue art – whether it be the art of writing or any other. The primary reason for this is that Lewis saw all human creativity as derivative rather than genuinely original, all of it ultimately being a reflection of God's creativity. A second reason for believing this is that a particular strand of Victorian thinking, exemplified by the poet Matthew Arnold, had, in a previous generation, begun to raise 'culture' to a quasi-religious status. A high level of knowledge and sensitivity to literature, painting or music, was seen as having a purifying effect upon the soul, lifting one above the masses unable to appreciate them.[7] Not only did Lewis deplore the snobbishness of this, he saw too that it was a false god and one that was destructive of the very thing it claimed to elevate. This view can be found in Lewis's writing on Literary Theory, but also in his 1956 address on **Sir Walter Scott** (1771-1832) whose novels he loved and re-read many times. Scott's Romanticism, and his fondness for the Medieval and Renaissance periods appealed strongly to him.

---

7 In writing about one of Shelley's poems, Lewis describes it as a happy rebuke to the new Puritanism which captured in particular many Cambridge critics in the 1950s and 1960s who objected to finding pleasure in poetry simply because it was pleasure.

C.S. LEWIS ON LITERATURE

It may not have occurred to every reader that the way we think about the past now is not as it always was. Lewis states, on good authority, that it is to Scott that we owe a way of thinking about the past that is properly historical. This is now widely accepted. For two centuries we have owed Scott the debt of knowing that the past is 'a foreign country' where things were done differently. However, this view is unacceptable to some in today's culture and Scott himself is subject to censure for Islamophobia in *Ivanhoe*. Such a view of this great writer is a mistake: in *The Talisman* he admires the Islamic leader Saladin and depicts the crusades as deeply misconceived.

Lewis's main concern, however, is the objection that Scott was insufficiently 'serious' about his work and he examines three ways in which that might, or might not, be true. One of these ways is to look at the claim that Scott disobeyed his artistic conscience. But, says Lewis, Scott knew only one kind of conscience, the one that demanded that he pay off his debts even if the books that helped him do it were less good than he wanted. Lewis pretends that he is not the person able to judge whether all previous ages were wrong in making art subordinate to life, or whether the modern world rates art too highly, but in reality his strongly-held view is abundantly clear.

In the past, he argues, artists were employed in entertaining people, in beautifying public events and places or in teaching 'virtue'. To raise the artist's status above this work will be to lose the prodigal carelessness of art we see in a Chaucer or Dickens figure. To enjoy rather than exert your genius, as Scott did, to make it 'play' rather than place it on a pedestal, is to put first things first.

HIS LITERARY CRITICISM, HISTORY, THEORY

The other factor that betrays Lewis's seemingly dispassionate and academic tone here is his treatment of a critic who cynically misconstrues (as jealousy) the motive of a Scott heroine who nobly refuses to commit perjury. To read such a review, he says, is as if one were reading the views of "a jackal on a book written by a lion." It is the bitterest comment about a critic that he published. In the end he chooses to pity such people who are the victims of an age of 'barbarism'. It is a measure of how far we have changed in the twenty-first century that the 1950s look now to us like an age of comparative innocence.

This defence of Scott's 'insufficient seriousness' is an application of the principle we see in Lewis's "Christianity and Literature" – that seriousness is not a necessary criterion for excellence and 'artistic conscience' not an adequate replacement for conscience. Lewis does suggest a possible 'middle view' that art is, or can be, serious but the moment the artist discovers this its value is lost – just as Eros had to flee when Psyche turned a lantern on to him. 1956 was both the year of this address and of the publication of *Till We Have Faces*, his novel which re-tells the myth of Cupid and Psyche. Again, Lewis's criticism and his fiction are exploring the same human propensities to vanity and curiosity – though of course his novel transmutes the myth into a study in self-deception.

Putting second things first, corrupts them. Art is no exception. Lewis states this as a universal law, and of course it is the biblical principle underlying the First Commandment. It is the cause of the fall and all subsequent history in Christian terms. There are examples in other Lewis works where he shows that not only corruption stems from this but also a quenching of joy. That lack of joy impacts on how we treat others and is a contributory cause to the whole of humanity's social failure.

C.S. LEWIS ON LITERATURE

UNDECEPTIONS: FICTION WHICH PROVIDES 'A MOMENT OF TRUTH' AND A CONSEQUENT 'AWAKENING'.

Jane Austen (1775-1817) is among the best known and best loved of all novelists writing in English in the last two centuries. Completing only six novels in her short life, and publishing those anonymously, meant that even her epitaph in Winchester Cathedral did not refer to her genius as a novelist. It was not until the later nineteenth and earlier twentieth centuries that she received serious academic attention. Even now opinion is divided but her popular success in both America and Britain has never been greater with many film and television adaptations of her work.

Lewis chooses *Northanger Abbey, Sense and Sensibility, Pride and Prejudice*, and *Emma*, and notes that each describes a distinct moment of 'awakening' in the heroines' lives. In *Sense and Sensibility* because Marianne Dashwood's awakening is so near to tragedy there is in the vocabulary used a note unfamiliar in Austen: a note bringing to the fore the underlying "religious background of the author's ethical position". (Lewis quotes: *penitence, amendment, self-destruction, my God* as examples.) These moments of undeception in the novels, suffered with varying degrees of pain, show the heroines the extent of the mistakes they have made about themselves and their world. Re-interpretation of all data in the mind of the character has then to take place and yet, there is a strong similarity of process shared by all four: the deception was caused by factors *within themselves*. Moreover, the moment of undeception is the turning-point of the story.[8] Such a pattern means that in an important sense they have but one plot between them.

---

8 All these points apply to the 'heroine' or central character of *Till We Have Faces*.

HIS LITERARY CRITICISM, HISTORY, THEORY

Lewis is not pointing this out as an authorial fault but rather, it would seem, as a realisation about human nature, and about the age that each society necessarily inhabits. He also points to the fact that Austen makes sense of the world through great classical abstract nouns and concepts: *courage, contentment, fortitude; vanity, folly, ignorance,* are some of those he quotes. This is not harshness by Austen but clarity of vision, realism and good sense. The hardness is reserved for *oneself* in the novels, not for one's neighbour. And it is this framework of morality, perhaps even of religion, says Lewis, that makes good comedy possible. They are the norm, the "seriousness" from which we deviate to provide comedy and irony. If everything is ironic, comedy will be frustrated. To spell this out (as Lewis of course does not here), the fact that we hold a particular worldview (in this case that there is a moral law that can be transgressed) always impacts on an individual's behaviour. As we believe, so we act.

Once again, the theological echoes are apparent. Lewis has seen that Austen has put her finger on the universal human condition and that we need to be awakened from the egotistical spell we have fallen under. In that sense, there is only one story to be told, only 'one plot' in all our lives: how, when, or whether, we awake, or not. Everyone's story is different, and yet in another sense, everyone's is the same in its beginning and middle parts. It is the conclusion that will differ or distinguish us: how we react to the moment of truth. It is no coincidence that this 1954 essay was written during the same period that he was writing the Narnia stories which begin with that country being discovered under a spell that Aslan will remove. Other stories such as *The Horse and His Boy* also play with the idea of spells and how they transform the way we see things.

C.S. LEWIS ON LITERATURE

Most readers today would miss the detail of why Marianne Dashwood's undeceiving is different from that of the other heroines and not give any conscious thought to what lies behind this and its implications. Lewis provides this insight which greatly enriches our appreciation of Jane Austen's work. It may be comedy but underlying it are truths about ourselves that most of her critics miss.

If there is but 'one plot' in these four Jane Austen novels, it could be argued that there is also only one in Lewis's fiction –and that too centres on undeception, on the process of 'awakening'. Leading examples of this are Orual in *Till We Have Faces*[9] and Mark Studdock in *That Hideous Strength*. We might say that this is a repeated motif running the whole length of his fiction; but the imaginative worlds he creates, unlike Austen's, are widely dissimilar from each other in both space and time. Moreover, his characters are highly individualised in their nature, background and setting. His science-fiction trilogy and *Till We Have Faces*, the Narnia stories and his short stories, all reveal the extent of this variety. Unlike the Austen heroines discussed, some of Lewis's central figures, presented with an opportunity for 'awakening' choose not to take it, thereby bringing the 'serious' element sharply into focus. *Undeceptions*[10] is the title Walter Hooper chose for a large collection of Lewis's essays. Many of them exemplify how he was frequently trying to provide his readers with experiences, either imaginative or intellectual, which were designed to 'undeceive' his readers, to bring us out from the 'enchantment' of twentieth century assumptions or falsehoods. His novels and stories, however, exemplify some characters who have already broken (or will break)

---

9 Orual realises that she had never selflessly loved Psyche (see p.317) despite her protestations to the contrary (see p.296).

10 *Undeceptions* is out of print, but all the essays it comtained and more are available in *God in the Dock*.

that spell – though still subject to its temptations. *The Screwtape Letters*[11] combine fiction (strictly speaking, epistolary fiction) with theology and apologetics in a way that shows the spiritual forces behind both the creation and the breaking of that spell on a daily basis. Once more, Lewis's output is all of a piece: criticism, fiction, apologetics cohere around the essential realities of our experience. Nothing we encounter is entirely trivial: we all have roles in the grandest and most truly mythical drama of all.[12] [13]

---

[11] This was the only book Lewis admitted that he did not enjoy writing. See *God in the Dock* (Eerdmans, 1970) p.219

[12] Ransom finds himself "enacting a myth" in *Perelandra* (p. 52, Ch. 4) and later realises that what might be mythical in one planet or world might be factual in another. (p.115, Cgh. 8)

[13] Criticism on Morris, Scott, and Austen may be found in *Selected Literary Essays*

C.S. LEWIS

Selected Literary Essays

Cambridge University Press

CHAPTER THREE

THE 18TH AND 17TH CENTURIES:
TOWARDS THE END OF THE OLD WESTERN WORLD

In one of his most famous addresses Lewis described himself as a dinosaur.[1] It was a term that some chose to mock. Even Joy Davidman, later to be his wife, while loving the brilliant and "intellectually exciting" lecture, described his description of post-Christian Europe as "rather previous of him"[2]. But events have proved Lewis to be right. Few saw more clearly than he that his concluding sentence, "There are not going to be many more dinosaurs" referred to the fact that though there would be more Christians, there would be few who grew up with an unbroken tradition, a line of DNA as it were, that would enable them to understand instinctively or by sympathetic scholarship the great assumptions of the European or 'Old Western' Christian world.

This combination of brilliant scholarship and faith enabled Lewis to see what others missed in the 1950s but which now, in the twenty-first century, is far more apparent. Namely, that the gap between the Christian and post-Christian worlds is a far deeper fissure than that between the pre-Christian or Pagan world and the world of the entire Christian era. Today it is commonplace for figures in public life, those in academia, the mass of ordinary consumers and, of course, children in school to have no recognition of the source of Biblical allusion, the basics of Christian doctrine or the expectations of Christian ethics. They, and we therefore as a society, are year on year increasingly cut off from the source,

---

1 "De Descriptione Temporum" reprinted in *Selected Literary Essays*, Ed. Walter Hooper (Cambridge University Press, 1969)

2 Quoted in Colin Duriez, *The C. S. Lewis Encyclopedia* (Azure Press, 2002) p. 150

and have lost many of the customary behaviours established in the Christian period.

The watershed of change is, for most people, the Enlightenment period, the eighteenth century. The very word "enlightenment" speaks volumes: the end of being benighted or lost in the dark; the dawn of the Age of Reason as opposed to faith or superstition. It is a concept which has been frequently doubted in more recent times, but Lewis's judgement was already that this period was not the Great Divide. Rather, that came early in the nineteenth century, after Jane Austen, and could be seen supremely in the invention of machines but also in religion, politics and the arts.

The process (Lewis relates) had begun, however, much earlier in terms of ideas even though these did not filter through to wider society. He places the essayist **Joseph Addison** (1672-1719) – whom he calls "historically momentous" – at the beginning of the period which was, he believed, just coming to a close in his day, in which it became possible and then normal to speak not of orthodoxy and heresy, but of people being religious or otherwise. There was, in other words, a distancing, a coolness, which enabled thinkers and writers to regard matters of faith as that which *others* experienced, as a phenomenon, not as a 'given' of common human life. Almost suddenly, the jokes in Shakespeare about works and faith, or Puritans and Catholics, were in danger of being misunderstood or altogether missed. What started to replace these assumptions was Rational Piety: the unexamined feeling that there are certain things one does (church on Sunday for instance) which keep one on the right side of the Deity; the sense that religion is all a bit of a mystery and that too much enthusiasm about it is rather distasteful.

HIS LITERARY CRITICISM, HISTORY, THEORY

At the same time that this thinking gradually developed, Lewis reminds us that another "profound change in human sentiment" was occurring: the Romantic Movement. This might not seem of much relevance to the ordinary reader today who has no interest in literary history but a wide study of Lewis's writing would suggest otherwise. For it was the Romantics who changed not only how we see the world but how we see ourselves, art, and ultimately God. It is helpful for thinking Christians to be able to recognise this. Lewis reminds us that prior to the Romantics the things in nature which people enjoyed excluded places of wildness or waste or darkness or danger – mountains, dense forests, waterfalls, rocky coasts.

Many students of literature will know this but Lewis notes that Addison moves these places out of the 'unpleasant' category and into a class of "the Great". This is a sort of half-way house to the Beautiful, and similar to Edmund Burke's famous later distinction between the Sublime and the Beautiful (1757). But it is Addison who is on the very cusp of this profound change – made possible partly by the growing sense of security that bourgeois writers at least were able to enjoy, freer as they were than ever before from the terrors and threats of the natural world with larger, safer houses, better roads and better sanitation. Why is this important for intellectually curious Christians to know? Lewis does not spell this out here but readers of his work on Literary Theory will recognise it as part of his approach to all literary study and integral to his worldview.

As the Romantic Movement, often dated in poetry from the time of William Blake (1757-1827) – also thought of as a precursor to the main figures – grew, it was increasingly the view both of poets and public to see the artist not as someone employed to entertain and delight, or a person especially gifted in capturing the glories of

God's creation, a sort of signpost to another world, but as a much more highly elevated figure who attracted attention to himself. His art therefore was less of a craft and more of an aesthetic, and eventually quasi-religious, experience. This became explicit in the Victorian period – and its progeny, Lewis felt, surrounded him in English Faculties, especially in Cambridge. That view of writing, of art in general, changes not only how the world sees art but how we see ourselves and God. The creativity in the Universe has moved from God to Man. Women and men no longer reflect a greater Beauty (God's) but *originate* it. In this respect the "Old Western" view of the world has been turned topsy-turvy; God is pushed to the margins (if acknowledged at all), and gratitude for life is exchanged for complaint that this central person – who I am – sometimes has their 'rights' disregarded. The 'selfie' age today is its grandchild. Our current world illustrates very exactly Lewis's principle that overvaluing art leads to its loss. Today, instead of marvelling at the *Mona Lisa*, tourists photograph themselves standing in front of it – with the aim that their friends should marvel not at the picture but at *them*. The result is a sort of hierarchy of competing vanities rather than the humility which the proper appreciation of great art should give rise to. There will be more to say about this when we examine Lewis's contributions to Literary Theory.

When we go back to the previous century we find ourselves breathing the air of a world still suffused with Christian belief: the world of Bunyan's *The Pilgrim's Progress*, of Milton's *Paradise Lost* and of the Authorised Version, or 'King James' Bible (1611). It is in these fertile but complex fields of study that Lewis could spread his wings with the greatest authority. Not only had his adult life been spent teaching and reading the literature, but his Christian mindset and experience enabled him to understand and roam freely inside a world that others could only look at from *out*side.

HIS LITERARY CRITICISM, HISTORY, THEORY

None of the three texts mentioned above is easy to read today, though those brought up on the 1611 translation of the Bible will have found that familiarity (in that case) overcomes, or disguises, most difficulties. In the case of **John Bunyan** (1628-1688), his famous book, which has never been out of print, was second only to the Bible in popularity throughout nineteenth-century America and Britain. But both its length and the genre of allegory can deter readers. Lewis was, arguably, the world's most learned reader of allegorical literature. His first major book was a study of it and he was still writing and speaking about allegory in his final years. It is a genre about as far removed from the focus and intentions of the 'selfie' age as it is possible to get. Lewis described it in his Preface to *The Pilgrim's Regress* (1933) as being the medium which exists not to hide things but to reveal them and a means of making our inner or spiritual worlds more real. Allegory is therefore, I suggest, instructive for Christians today as it points away from the superficial, the photographic, the merely visual, by making its visible fictional characters represent invisible spiritual, mental (or even physical) human experience.

Bunyan's great book, however, is not without its faults, Lewis tells us. Some of the dialogues between Christian and Hopeful are too long and are liable to send the average reader to sleep. The dialogue with Mr Talkative is worse still. Moreover, in places the allegory dissolves and the text becomes sermonical which renders the allegory irrelevant. The story disappears behind the pulpit. But the fault is rare; Bunyan is an exemplar of "perfect naturalness" in his characters' speech and we are given an unadorned adventure story full of giants and goblins, spells, dungeons and castles. In that respect, the book, we might now say, was the seventeenth-century equivalent of *Harry Potter* but with a much deeper application being both intended and recognised. It is full of homely familiar images too: gossipy neighbours, snobs, children up to no good, family life, illness and doctors.

This mixture of homeliness and far-reaching profundity enables Lewis to draw a parallel with parables in the gospels which interpreters, he reminds us, often disregard. Working like allegory, they give us "one thing in terms of another". The prodigal son story, with all its earthiness about greed, envy, pigs and prostitutes concludes with a new outfit of clothes and a huge meal – a party. The application of this is not stated but left for us to reflect on. But the son is not rewarded with merely spiritual consolement. Allegory is not a code to be translated into the language of abstraction. The physical details are important because the whole point of allegory, Lewis goes on to explain, is not, for example, to think, "this green valley I've read about is representative of humility" but just the reverse: that humility is like the green valley: it's a beautiful and fruitful place to be. In that way, moving away from the concept (humility) and towards the image (the green valley) we understand more about the concept. Here again, we find Lewis revivifying our reading of Scripture in the midst of a quite academic address first read over BBC radio (1962) and therefore not to a targeted Christian audience. It is all part of his integrated approach to reading anything – 'religious' or secular.

As an aside at this point, Lewis passes on some advice to all would-be writers, Christian or not. Sincerity is not enough – though Bunyan, pot mender, common soldier and son of a pot mender, would probably have believed this, and had himself no literary pretensions. Sincerity is a virtue, a moral attribute, not a literary one. The inference is that the ability to write well is a skill, an art, to be learned. Lewis gives the example of his work as a censor of soldiers' letters during World War One. Utterly sincere as the letters of many ordinary men were, they were full of platitude and cliché. This is one of the very few times we hear Lewis mention his role in that conflict (outside *Surprised by Joy*) which he largely excised from his memory. Indeed, he tells us in his 1955 autobiography that it felt as if his wartime experiences had happened to someone else, that they were cut off from the rest of life.³

Lewis then briefly tackles another topic which might prevent a modern reader from persevering with Bunyan: the narrowness of his religious viewpoint, its sectarianism, and its intolerance of others. This is worth drawing our attention to for it is often a source of deep complaint against the Church of this period in particular. The first thing to note in its defence, we are told, is that all our forebears wrote and spoke in that forthright and damning manner when defending a teaching, so "historical allowances" can perhaps be made.⁴ In our current climate that should be easy enough to believe since we see astonishing intolerance by secular public figures (now more so than Christian ones) of anyone who dares to gainsay a trending opinion. The vitriol expressed over social media is in no sense more restrained than writings of previous ages. How will future ages perceive our own? The evidence that those ages were thus severe in many respects (not just religion), I would also add, is readily available in their penal codes and statute books – neither being the product of the Church but of the ruling authority – whether monarch or parliament. Bunyan himself was incarcerated merely for his views and wrote *The Pilgrim's Progress* from prison.

There is, however, for many an even more objectionable side

---

3 *Surprised By Joy*, (Geoffrey Bles, 1955) p.185

4 G. K. Chesterton makes the point well about such matters in earlier centuries: "They fought because they had something to fight about. It is easy enough to be refined about things that do not matter." *All Things Considered* (Methuen, 1908) p.45

to Bunyan that might deter wider readership; it is what Lewis calls "the intolerable terror". Bunyan chose to conclude Part I of the book with Pilgrim noticing "that there was a way to Hell, even from the Gates of Heaven, as well as from the City of *Destruction.*" This is indeed a frightening doctrine but Lewis looks at it as a literary element which underlines the urgency and momentous nature of Pilgrim's journey. Without this constant reminder Lewis felt the book would lose power to an immeasurable degree. A Christian reader today is thereby presented with the question as to what extent in the proclamation of a 'saving' gospel some awareness of the alternative is essential for it to retain its power. Has the loss of the concept of Hell in many quarters contributed to the weakness of the Church? We know from *The Great Divorce* and *The Problem of Pain* (where he uses the same concept of the doctrine being intolerable[5] and yet a logical necessity), as well as other works, that Hell was not excluded from Lewis's thinking.[6]

Bunyan was born into an age which at the literary level was dominated by Scripture and at the political and theological levels by intolerance. An age of violent persecution had preceded it. William Tyndale, the greatest single contributor to the 1611 translation of the Bible, had been executed by other Christians for his beliefs which were seen as undermining Church authority. It was partly to reinforce that authority (and that of the monarch) that the **Authorised Version** was commissioned. In a 1950 lecture Lewis provided unusual insights to the translators' role, to the Bible itself and to its future usage.

> A good translation is more in debt to its original than any

---

5 *The Problem of Pain* (Geoffrey Bles, 1941) p.108

6 Reggie Weems, "Universalism Denied: C. S. Lewis' Unpublished letters to Alan Fairhurst", *Journal of Inklings Studies*, vol. 7/2, October 2017, 87-98

HIS LITERARY CRITICISM, HISTORY, THEORY

other factor that produced it and this is particularly true of narrative prose or instructions about morality. It is less true for lyric poetry but in the case of Hebrew poetry the frequent use of parallelism[7], "a translatable quality", means that this applies much less. As a result it is impossible to talk about the literary impact of the AV apart from the general impact of the Bible. The subject matter, the imagery, the figures all depend on the original manuscripts: the great stories of the Old Testament and the narratives in Acts, Lewis says, carry the weight they do irrespective of the variousness of the translations. He might surely have added the parables of Christ or the narrative passages of the Gospels. In all of literature there is nothing quite like Peter's denial, the cockcrow and Jesus's look at Peter in the fire-lit courtyard. What is shared by the originals and by every translation is so infinitely more important than their differences. It's an important point, because historically, and even today, churches can be split apart by favouring one translation over another. No translation can perfectly render the sense of the original throughout: no language is the exact counterpart of another. No good translation will be, uniformly and in every instance, a better translation than another good one.

A further major point that Lewis makes is to remind us (or perhaps more likely, tell many for the first time) that although the first Protestant translators shed the allegorising tendencies of the Middle Ages and the elaborative nature of the Renaissance approach, every tradition is dependent on another. English and European traditions in translation transcend national boundaries and most of the variants are made not for doctrinal reasons but as a result of advances in linguistic studies, in philology. William

---

7 That is, the device of saying the same thing in two ways, or in which a second line presents the opposite of the thought of the first, or develops it. It is especially strong in the Psalms, e.g., Psalms 2:4 and 37:6 (see *Reflections on the Psalms*), Introductory chapter.

Tyndale accepted correction from Thomas More and it is possible to trace changes which may have started in the Geneva Bible, that were then received in Rheims and from there reached the Authorised Version. We stand on each other's shoulders, and the realisation of that breeds not only civility but unity. But Lewis clearly reserves a very high place for Tyndale – "the best prose writer of his age".

What of the Bible's future? It is here that Lewis's views, rather bleak as they are, seem particularly prescient. More than seventy years on from the date at which this lecture was penned we have a post-Christian world from which all but a handful of Biblical phrases and ideas have been lost to the majority of people – as far as any knowledge of their place of origin is concerned. We have moved a long way from a society which for three hundred years and more was so suffused with Biblical language that hardly a word or expression could be lifted without it being recognised. You might use the word profanely or piously, Lewis writes, but you could not use it neutrally. At school or home or at church the text would have been read. But in the third decade of the twenty-first century, in most social gatherings of younger people in Europe, if not in America, the allusion will not be picked up. Basic knowledge of the Bible has vanished in two generations. The cause is not just ignorance, but antipathy and Lewis is useful in explaining why. The first antipathy is that the Bible has not always been the literary pleasure to read that we imagine. We have seen that the Romantic Movement steadily grew through the eighteenth century. During that time tastes changed and the exotic, the elemental, our passion for primitive or simple things in nature and in stories grew too. The Old Testament reverberates with such stories and Christ's parables and metaphors strike the same chord. As a result the Bible was seen as a literary phenomenon during that period. But Lewis lived through a "violently" anti-Romantic period, inimical to such

HIS LITERARY CRITICISM, HISTORY, THEORY

material and unlikely to prompt any 'literary' readings. In its place today is a trend equally concerning: a political correctness, a fear of 'appropriation' and an age of 'trigger warnings' for the slightest incursion into sensitive areas. The Bible, in all its parts, is seen by some as transgressing the new puritanism of perfect tolerance for all: a book to be 'cancelled', unfit for our present age. Lewis cites Moses and the Burning Bush, David and Absolom, the prophet Elijah on Mount Carmel, the Gadarene Maniac as examples of how antipathetic an anti-Romantic age would find the Bible stories. Today each of these and innumerable others might be found, by those determined to do so, to offend on grounds far more damaging than mere aestheticism.

Lewis's conclusion is that only when the religious claims of Scripture are once again recognised as having authority will the Bible regain a wider readership. It was brought together for a religious purpose and demands to be accepted on its own terms: it is unrelentingly sacred and a merely literary approach will not provide a sustained interest for any reader. Those who read it in future, as in the past, will almost all be Christians.[8]

---

8 Essays on Addison, Bunyan, and the Authorised Version may be found in *Selected Literary Essays*

CHAPTER FOUR

AN EPIC POEM MISUNDERSTOOD

John Milton (1608 -1674), growing up in the world of *The Authorised Version*, is the subject of one of Lewis's most brilliant and acclaimed books, *A Preface to Paradise Lost*. John V. Fleming (Emeritus Professor of English at Princeton) calls it his 'critical masterpiece'[1] and Dennis Danielson (Professor of English at University of British Columbia) calls it 'potent, compelling and eloquent'.[2] Contemporary opinion about the book included that of Nevill Coghill (Merton Professor of English at Oxford) who wrote that it was a 'magistral' work which along with Lewis's others led Coghill to conclude that he did "not know of any critic of our times who can equal this achievement."[3]

What Lewis wrote in 1942 about *Paradise Lost* remains revelatory for anyone interested in one of the greatest epic poems in English, but especially for Christians – whether students of literature or not. His teaching within his book's 139 pages illuminates not only how to read this poem so as to derive both deep spiritual and poetical sustenance from its vision of the created universe, but more particularly some unique insights to the fall, the character of Adam, the 'history' of Satan, the nature of literary study and our own human nature. Lewis expects of his readers that they will accept the mindset in which the epic was written and prepare for the imaginative impact of it as closely as the original readers would have – if we are to enter into the literary and cultural experience

---

   1   *The Cambridge Companion to C. S. Lewis*, Ed. Robert MacSwain and Michael Ward, (Cambridge University Press, 2010) p. 19
   2   Ibid. p.53
   3   *Light on Lewis*, Ed. J Gibb, (Geoffrey Bles, 1965) p. 65

available. Without an attempt at this, whatever else we get from the poem, it won't be what Milton was doing.

Milton was a Puritan intellectual and Cambridge graduate who pursued both a political and poetical career. He was prodigiously able and became an ardent Parliamentarian, rising to high office under Oliver Cromwell. In pamphlets he defended the right to expression free of censorship and the legitimacy of divorce. After the Restoration of the Monarchy (1660) he was arrested but eventually pardoned. In middle life he went totally blind and had to dictate his writings.

The twelve books of *Paradise Lost* tell the story of war in Heaven between Michael and the fallen angels led by Satan, Satan's banishment from Heaven[4] and God's creation of the world. The narrative goes on to depict the temptation and fall of Adam and Eve, their expulsion from Paradise and then Satan's further reduction and decline.

Because Milton suffered much misapprehension at that time (as he does now), Lewis's *Preface* seeks to explain much that was misconstrued, as much by students and academics as by more general readers. There is a wealth of spiritual food in the poetry for twenty-first-century readers but we need an expert guide to help us discover it. Lewis is that guide. The first principle in criticism, he tells us, as in so much, is to find out what something is designed to do – from a corkscrew to a cathedral. If we think a corkscrew is to open a tin we will not be saying anything useful about it. So he sets out to show us what *Paradise Lost* was designed to be: an *epic* poem.

---

[4] Lewis touches on this in *Perelandra* (pp.23-4, Chapter 2)

HIS LITERARY CRITICISM, HISTORY, THEORY
EPIC POETRY

The earliest (and oral) form of epic Lewis calls "Primary": it was to be recited in a noble and heroic court about a grave and tragic, apparently historical, set of events. The Greek poet Homer's two great poems, the *Odyssey* and the *Iliad,* are in this category. The recitation of these very long poems necessitated the use of repeated phrases or lines in order to allow the audience to keep up with the twist and turn of events, but also required Poetic Diction – an elevated unfamiliar style quite different from the everyday, avoiding the commonplace. The repeated "sonorous syllables" remind us that the predicament of uncertainty we all live under is a permanent and real pressure.

Lewis then goes on to speak of 'secondary epic'[5] and the Roman poet Virgil (70 – 19 BC) whose *Aeneid* takes a single national legend and makes it into "a transition in the world-order". Virgil, he tells us, universalizes the story of the founding of Rome into a conflict between duty and desire and the search for 'the abiding city'. The poem thereby becomes a symbol of the destiny of humanity.[6] The only development possible beyond this is for epic to have a subject which is overtly religious. A return to narrative that is *only* heroic would be anachronistic.

In this way, Lewis has shown his readers that in writing an epic poem Milton's elevated *style* is designed for the telling of an equally grave, tragic and grand story. Moreover, the story he tells, if it is to avoid anachronism, has to be, for Milton, the Christian

---

5 This new term became so well known that W. H. Auden used it without reference as the title of a poem. See *C. S. Lewis's lost Aeneid*, ed. A. T. Reyes (Yale University Press, 2011) p.9

6 Lewis claimed he read the *Aeneid* more often than any other long poem and saw in it the costliness of following a calling. Lewis could identify with such cost both in combat and in love – and perhaps also in his career. See A. T. Reyes, Op. Cit. pp. xviii and 11

account of God's cosmic plan.

The first lesson we can learn here, therefore, is that we should expect and *enjoy* the remote feel of the poem which is there to compensate for the fact that we have no palatial hall, no garlanded poet, no feast, no ritual, as the context for our reading is merely a book and an armchair at home. The style of Virgil and of Milton is compensatory; it counteracts the comparative privation of the solitary reader. It is entirely inept, a serious misjudgement, to blame the poet for achieving exactly what he intended to achieve. It would be like condemning an opera because the characters on stage were singing not speaking. The opening paragraph of the poem tells us that a great and elevated matter is about to unfold before our eyes. "Our very muscles" feel this sense, Lewis tells us. In today's world of film, we might say, it is the equivalent of sweeping camera work raising our expectations and anticipation as the credits roll at the start. Any "schoolboy" (as Lewis would have it) knowing nothing of Milton, but catching his breath as the initial lines open up a new world, is nearer to 'getting it' than critics who miss this.

His whole approach to the poem is an outstanding example of how Lewis, uniquely, managed to write objective literary criticism while at the same time defending both Milton's and his own intellectual position and Christian belief. In doing so he also exposes the flaws in the approach of other critics in ways which must have made them uncomfortable – and have been costly to him in terms of his acceptance within a mostly disbelieving set of colleagues.

Uncompromisingly, Lewis tackles the opposition head-on. How could they have missed what is so dazzlingly straightforward? Namely, the central moral that people are happy when they obey

HIS LITERARY CRITICISM, HISTORY, THEORY

God and miserable when they don't, as the essayist Addison had noted about the poem. It can only be because the idea is so disagreeable to modern critics that they have to pass it over or hush it up and focus on marginal issues.

THE DEPICTION OF SATAN

When it comes to the consideration of the most famous controversy, the 'character' of Satan in the poem, Lewis sets out to do battle with 150 years of adverse Milton criticism, "lost in misunderstanding" and inspired at least as much by revolutionary politics and the rejection of God, as by the poem. The eighteenth-century visionary poet, William Blake, believed that Milton was "of the Devil's party without knowing it". After this, Satan was seen as the most convincing character in the entire epic and having qualities that aroused the sympathy and admiration of readers – unlike the remoter figures of God and the Son. Lewis's *Preface* is concerned to re-educate an audience that would have largely shared this view. His first point is clarification of an ambiguity. Taking Miss Bates (a Jane Austen character) by way of example, he says she could be considered either as very entertaining or very dull. To read about her is entertainment; to be stuck with her in real life would be dull. So it is with Satan. If readers find him "magnificent" it may either mean we find the presentation of him an achievement of that order, or, if we were to meet him, that he would be "an object of admiration".

With devastating force Lewis then proceeds to show us what we are, or would be, admiring – as Milton presents him. First, he is a being suffering under "a sense of injur'd merit" – like a spoilt child or film star who is laughed at, until, that is, such time as they are able to cause hurt. Satan "thought himself impaired" because Messiah was proclaimed Head of the Angelic Host. Yet the appointment was made by his own Creator, with a perfect right to do so and with no slight intended. So, in a world full of glory and light and wonder Satan could think of nothing save his own status.[7]

John Milton

The dissection of Satan's character that follows – as it is in the poem – is vintage 'adversarial' Lewis who leaves no place to hide for those inclined to find Satan (rather than the poet's achievement in regard to him) admirable. The telling insights into human nature are also hardly comfortable, even for Christians who accept their own 'fallen' nature. Lewis shows us Milton's depiction of a Devil who is unceasingly intellectual but incapable of understanding anything. In saying "Evil be thou my good" he also condemns himself to "Nonsense be thou my sense". There must be many Christian readers today who perceive that sort of idiocy in not a

---

7 This is precisely what Weston's demonic ramblings indicate in *Perelandra* (p.147-8. Chapter 10).

HIS LITERARY CRITICISM, HISTORY, THEORY

few of the views of today's opinion makers. By Book IX of the poem Satan has become, of his own volition, a serpent. By Book X he *is* a serpent and without the choice of being otherwise. He then regresses from underworld spy to peeping Tom leering at Adam and Eve, intent on their harm simply in order to annoy the Enemy. He is then further changed to toad and finally to snake: such is Satan's "progress". Milton depicts this brilliantly but *what* he depicts is an object of complete contempt.

INSIGHTS TO HUMAN NATURE

But Lewis then draws our attention to something few articulate. Satan is Milton's best drawn character because it is far easier to make a fictional character *worse* than oneself than better; to do so we have only to release for a moment some of the badness which, in our own lives, is always "straining at the leash". If we do not have the "real high virtues" inside us then we can only show how they emanate in action, but not the root of their goodness; we can hardly explore what it is like to be that – it is beyond most of our imagining. In our present age we might add that it is often the film "villains" who are the most convincingly portrayed. But one further point is worth making here. Lewis's own creation of "good" fictional characters *is* powerful and convincing. Witness, in their quite different ways, Ransom and Aslan, the depiction of whom is therefore specially impressive.

Lewis not only dismantles Satan but is prepared to show Adam as far more interesting than many had allowed. Adam, he says, would be far better company than Satan just because of the variety of his conversation on topics as diverse as God, sleep, stars and planets, birds, the beauty of Eve and all the wonders of the Universe. Satan, by contrast, though he has witnessed these wonders – and far more - has found only one thing to talk about: himself. He is a "monomaniac".[8] In wishing to be himself, he has been granted just that by God and carries round with him "a hell of infinite boredom". It is a lesson Christians need to learn. In a 'selfie' age, our focus needs to be consciously turned outward, not in on ourselves. To give one's vote to Satan in the poem then is to wish for unceasing autobiography, lies and misery.

LEWIS'S UNIQUELY BOLD CONCLUSION

With rather astonishing directness, Lewis then effectively confronts the reader with this conclusion: that the careful reading of the poem produces a binary division between its readers. It was not what many colleagues would have wanted by way of an ending: we either love or hate the poem according to how we react to the exposure it forces upon us. We all have reasons to want to evade the poem's impact: the realisation that we are on one side or the other and moving always towards being more angelic or more devilish. "Each one of us", Lewis insists, is moving one way or the other.[9] The story of the poem is unlike any other, we are reminded, because it speaks of a real and irreversible process in our universe's history. Like the Great Wall of China it divides the farms of an ancient culture from the barbarism outside. If you see the wall from the wrong side, you hate it.

The book is, therefore, far more than just a "preface" to a uniquely great poem but is a defence of looking at literature in a particular way. For most of his career Lewis's criticism was

---

8 Lewis uses the same word of Weston on Perelandra in the last stages of demonic possession. (p.100, Chapter 7)

9 Ransom, in confronting the decay of Weston's being in *Perelandra* realises that each of us is inexorably heading towards either the "Beatific" vision or the "Miserific" (p.126, Chapter 9)

designed to oppose aspects of the views of the Cambridge critics I. A. Richards and F. R. Leavis. Leavis in particular promoted the idea of "literature as Truth" whereas Lewis wanted to demonstrate that literature *points us* to truth by delighting us in it as we respond to what we are shown.

There is, of course, so much more to *A Preface to Paradise Lost* than the few ideas I have included here. It is a great book in every sense. But these reflections and summaries may give readers unfamiliar with it, some small sense of its worth and offer an invitation to read it.[10]

---

[10] If there is a weakness to the book at all, it might be, as David Barratt suggested in a paper read to the UCCF Associates Literary Studies group, c. 1980, that Lewis's apologetic or defensive stance about the poem with its awareness of theological difficulties and the misunderstandings that moderns might suffer, might tend to deflect us from the poem itself and turn us to Lewis instead – which is the last thing he would have wanted.

HAMLET
THE PRINCE OR THE POEM?

BY
C. S. LEWIS

ANNUAL SHAKESPEARE LECTURE
OF THE
BRITISH ACADEMY
1942

CHAPTER FIVE

JOHN DONNE AND WILLIAM SHAKESPEARE

As we turn to poets who were born in the Elizabethan period it can be hard to avoid using the term 'Renaissance'. To do so is to touch upon an issue which was of central importance in Lewis's understanding of Western history. The term was one he used sparingly for reasons we shall make clear when we consider his contribution to Literary History. In general, the word is used to denote the (literary) period in which the sixteenth century was of central importance.

One figure of its later flowering who was of particular interest to Lewis was the English poet **John Donne** (1572-1631), born just eight years after Shakespeare. Neither his poetry nor Lewis's writing about it is an easy read but there are important points for readers today that Lewis makes when discussing his poetry.

While very much enjoying and admiring much of the poetry of John Donne, Lewis thought he was overrated. He saw his poetry not so much as innovative but as a continuation and development of an earlier 'plain' and 'manly' style – predictably more attractive to the mid- twentieth century than the 'mellifluous' and 'luxurious' tone often found in the earlier poets, Philip Sidney and Edmund Spenser – the latter a favourite for Lewis. Today, as well as being entertaining and provocative, Donne has much to offer in his religious poetry. Some of his sonnets (for example *Death Be Not Proud*) can produce a deep joy and be a real stimulus to faith for those who delight in words so precisely crafted. In his essay "Donne and Love Poetry in the Seventeenth Century" (1938) Lewis calls some of the love poems "extremely affecting"; he would have said the same of the divine poems had the essay been on that topic.

C.S. LEWIS ON LITERATURE

We are reminded in the essay that all of us are subject to the fashions and preconceptions of our own age – a constant in Lewis's writing. Donne, instead of using images from the natural world like his predecessors, frequently drew on topical issues – urban life, the sciences, law or philosophy, thus immediately offering a familiar foothold to the mid-twentieth century with its preference for 'realism' and 'kitchen sink' drama. Donne is also introspective and cynical, and something of a literary 'show-off' – all habits of thought strongly marked in Lewis's day as well as now. Donne's day and that of Lewis both occurred at the end of an obviously noble poetic period which allowed an easy sympathy between the two in their reaction against it. The lesson therefore to be learned is that an intellectual fashion or fad, a taste for certain ideas, art or literature is part of the 'chronological snobbery'[1] that tends to mislead us into thinking that whatever is current is somehow better than whatever went before. Donne may be suited to our tastes now, Lewis suggests, but that has no bearing on whether he was a better poet than others or the truth of what he had to show us. Christians, as well as general readers and students of literature, constantly need to be on their guard against being deceived by the latest ideas (including the desire to be thought clever) which may not be supported by the facts. We are most easily deceived by those assumptions which are so commonplace that hardly anyone dare question them. Assumptions about the origins of life and matter, about morality, about the Bible and the Church have all undergone reversals in the last 150 years to a degree which means they are

---

1 Lewis mentions this in *Surprised by Joy*, and that he was cured of it by Owen Barfield. He was scathing about it in a BBC broadcast on the novels of Charles Williams where he calls our assumptions of superiority to the past "fatuous" yet certain to dominate unless we take steps to correct them. See C. S. Lewis, *C. S. Lewis on Stories and Other Essays on Literature,* Ed. Walter Hooper (Harcourt Brace Jovanovich 1982)p. 50. Moreover, the more anxious we are to be contemporary, the more likely we are to be quickly "dated". Ibid. p. 149

hard to challenge in many quarters even though some of them are intellectually risible.

Lewis then continues by pointing out a widespread misconception about the relative positions of Puritans and Roman Catholics in Donne's day on matters of morality. That misconception, namely that the Catholics were indulgent liberals and the Puritans severe and restrictive, lingers on today in some circles. It was the Puritans who had 'the easy doctrine' Lewis tells us.[2] To realise this affects not only our understanding of Donne in general, but in particular of his treatment of love (a major theme) and the tendency within the Protestant faith to be slightly smug about our relation to the past Roman Catholic communion. Our assumption, born of later conceptions (not least our perception of Calvin's theocracy in Geneva), is that the Puritans of the sixteenth century were, what we understand by the word, 'puritanical'. It will come as a surprise to many that Lewis has to correct this with a firm hand and lets us know that Luther himself, as much the Catholic Sir Thomas More, would be equally shocked by the mistake. In terms of their view of marriage, the Puritans were far more indulgent than the Catholics, nor were they necessarily ascetic in other matters. The sourness often attributed to Puritans which is contrasted with a defence of 'merry' England by the Catholics is the reverse of the case in the age under discussion. The doctrine of salvation by faith, without the penance or mortification that the older Church demanded was seen by them as something too easy, a fool's paradise perhaps. Luther's writing and speaking was extremely free and easy, disregarding scruples a Catholic might have. But his attitude to women is much more accepting and positive than More's. Precise correctness in every matter is seldom

---

2 Donne was 'bred' a Catholic but Lewis does not mention he was ordained into the Church of England in 1615.

to be found on one side of a historical argument. Let us not be too judgemental of our forebears.

When it comes to passing judgement on Donne's love poetry Lewis is unequivocal that despite its many merits, the poetry can only interest most readers for a limited time and in a rather superficial way. The complexity of the poems is more of an intellectual conundrum than the ambiguities born out of experience. More conventional poets could show us more of why they write about this matter of love, more of the substance of this emotion that engulfs men and women the world over. And here it is that we discover another profound principle about the way Lewis approaches all varieties of human experience. Donne was only able to write as he did because there existed already a tradition, a norm, from which he departed. The shadows he drew could not exist without the overarching sun. Unless there is a standard by which we judge things, nothing can be judged to be, literally, extraordinary, or out-of-the-ordinary, for there would be no *ordinary* from which to depart. Lewis uses this argument with regard to natural law in his ethical writings and his whole approach as to how we can make sense of anything has this as one of its foundations. As he says in his apologetic works, if no things are self-evident, then nothing we say about human perceptions can be proved. The principle applies whoever your audience, whatever your topic, whatever the age.

Lewis did not consider himself a **Shakespeare** (1564-1616) specialist but the poet was one he was familiar with from childhood, for his fame has of course outstripped every other writer in the Western literary tradition. More has been written about Shakespeare's work than perhaps any other poet in history. His histories, comedies, tragedies and romances have generated a world-wide industry of criticism and performance. Rather little is

HIS LITERARY CRITICISM, HISTORY, THEORY

known of his personal life and the origin of his genius remains one of the great mysteries of the literary world.

His plays captured Lewis's imagination and though he never wrote a book about Shakespeare, in 1939 he published an essay: "Variation in Shakespeare and Others." Among other things it is a passport to being able to attend a performance of any the plays, or to reading the text, in a way few of us, if any, will ever have done before. Another essay, "Hamlet, The Prince or the Poem?" (1942) began life as the Annual Shakespeare Lecture to the British Academy. It sheds light both on Shakespeare's life and one of Lewis's recurring themes. We will look at the Variation essay first.

The term 'variation' is of course in common usage but Lewis means here something very specific by it: namely, the repetition of metaphors about a single idea, a convention which predominates in the Elizabethan dramatists. We find it in the parallelism[3] of the Psalms and to some extent in all poetry. But here he focuses much on *Macbeth* and *Hamlet* – two widely familiar plays – and begins by asking what was the playwright's distinct contribution to our poetry? Not perhaps a question that many of us will have asked, and fewer still will have answered. Lewis, however, is in no doubt: it is the combination, to an extraordinary degree, of the ability to create the very finest sort of imaginative lyric poetry with the presentation of human character, human daily life, with the highest degree of realism. Many writers in prose and poetry can do one or the other; no one else does both as Shakespeare does. Lewis then adds to this verdict by stating that this combination depends precisely on *variation*. It's a fascinating insight which opens up

---

3 That is, the device of saying the same thing in two ways, or in which a second line presents the opposite of the thought of the first, or develops it. It is especially strong in the Psalms. E.g. Psalm 24 vv. 1-2

swathes of text to an entirely new light of understanding.

The problem Shakespeare found a solution to was that "real passion" does not express itself well. If his characters, undergoing as they do the greatest of emotional tests, were to speak as real people speak, their language would not reveal any depths of character – which is what is so compelling about them. If, however, they speak only in high-flown and perfect verse the reality of their suffering, their joy, their other strong emotions, will not reach us. 'Variation', Lewis discovers, is Shakespeare's (possibly unconscious) path through this seemingly intractable problem. He gives examples – lines which when read in the light of this perception transform both how the actor should deliver the lines and how the audience should hear them.

A brilliant example cited by Lewis occurs shortly after the murder of Duncan in *Macbeth*, as Macbeth struggles to express what he has done:

> Methought I heard a voice cry 'sleep no more!
> Macbeth does murder sleep', the innocent sleep,
> Sleep that knits up the ravell'd sleeve of care,
> The death of each day's life, sore labour's bath,
> Balm of hurt minds, great nature's second course,
> Chief nourisher in life's feast.

The metaphors here, instead of being seen as part of a showy, wordy, declamation should be seen as "words thrown off accidentally" as the character under intense duress searches almost blindly for something that will express what he means, be adequate to the emotion racking him, be an escape valve for the passions tearing at him.

Macbeth could have said only one of these things about sleep

HIS LITERARY CRITICISM, HISTORY, THEORY

and it would have been one of the greatest lines on the matter ever written, but if he had, we would not have believed him, Lewis explains. As it is, Macbeth has no time to reflect on what he has said in his agony and we, the audience, only later come to realise that these lines were great and moving poetry. In the performance, they are the utterances of a despairing, disbelieving, remorseful weakling from whom we shrink in horror. It is, as Lewis uniquely noted, 'variation' that allows this. Lewis has discovered for us a defining mark of Shakespeare's genius and shown how the poet 'gets through' to his audience.

To any one recovering from bad teaching of the bard at school, or bad performances anywhere, Lewis has opened a door to further understanding, empathy and delight in all the plays.

Earlier, when discussing John Bunyan, we had occasion to refer to our current age of the 'selfie' photograph and culture. In Lewis's essay on *Hamlet* he brings to the fore his prime concern in reading which we shall meet later in his work on Literary Theory: his insistence that 'self' has to be got out of the way as we allow ourselves to be subjected to the work in hand. For Lewis this is the first principle of all reading. It is also, as we know from his religious writing a first principle in life; the negation of self, the dying to self that is the key to life and a core element of Christ's teaching. We shall also see here his view that literary criticism can, likewise, inhibit our responses by interposing itself between us and the text.

In a rare piece of self-revelation Lewis tells us that "the meddlers" or critics he read in his teens disenchanted him by insisting that the witches, and thunder and lightning (which he loved) at the start of *Macbeth* were not the really interesting things. Rather, the interest was only in the effect of the witches on the King's character. Similarly, the critics tell him, at the start of *Twelfth Night* it is not the spell-like charm of the music and golden syllables that should fascinate but the portrayal of a fantasising Duke (Orsino) who needed psychiatric treatment, or at least diagnosis. After these telling examples of wrong-headed criticism, Lewis clinches his opening salvo with two magnificent lines from *Richard II* in which the King cannot even banish a man save by saying:

> The sly slow hours shall not determinate
> The deathless limit of thy dear exile.[4]

    Such lines are simply to drink in and be thankful, Lewis explains, and are part of the romance of how wilful, impassioned kings doomed in years long gone by ought to speak. They are perfect. But no, the critic deflects us from them by "instilling the pestilential notion" that they are there to show up Richard's weakness and the "efficiency" of Bolingbroke, his (temporary) victim. The result of this was that Lewis, seriously put off, only came back to Shakespeare when he learnt to read him *another way*. It is a reminder to us that there are different ways of reading the same text, and that some are better than others. Whether it be the Bible or books of a quite different kind, if we are not usefully finding what others do, we may need to change our viewpoint or our spectacles. The right way with Shakespeare, Lewis tells us, is to surrender to the situation of the plot and to the magic of the poetry, and in that way come to the characters. All else is liable to lead up a blind alley or one that leads us only back to ourselves rather than the "bright shapes" from the mind of the poet. As soon as we bring a superior self to the poetry, that 'self' starts to find insincerities in the verse that the genius of the poet did not intend. We are not in the theatre to reduce the poetic vision to banality or the commercial "philosophy of …Henry Ford."

---

    4 *Richard II*, I iii 150

HIS LITERARY CRITICISM, HISTORY, THEORY

In my experience, 'Shakespeare studies' at school and university often contradict this approach and can make reading the plays a very sterile experience. Lewis seeks to revive in his readers the immediacy of the impact of the story at a first reading and to retain that freshness wherever possible.

Lewis's 1942 lecture "Hamlet: The Prince or the Poem?" is related to his earlier one in one obvious way, and one rather less obvious. In it, he is still concerned to part company with those who dismiss the opening scene with its numinous ghost as a mere mechanism for launching the revenge plot – Hamlet's struggle to avenge his father's murder by his usurping uncle. As with the witches, Lewis sees this scene as inseparable from the intrinsic nature of the play which is about a man tasked by a ghost to act. That is the single most important thing about the figure. The darkness, fear and cold of the opening scene on the battlements of Elsinore, and the suspense of it, make the play what it is. Without this, it would be radically changed. Lewis challenged his listeners at this point to disagree if they could, so certain was he of his ground.

Having established the centrality of the ghost, a visitor from the afterlife, to his conception of the play, Lewis drops into the turbulent waters of *Hamlet* criticism his direction-changing assertion: "the subject of *Hamlet* is death."[5] From this point on, the less than obvious connection with the earlier essay and with so much of Lewis's thinking begins to become apparent. He has

---

5   In this respect, Shakespeare is closely linked to Donne: "Donne saw, analysed, lived alongside, even saluted corruption and death. He was often hopeless, often despairing, and yet still he insisted at the very end: it is an astonishment to be alive, and it behoves you to be astonished." Rundell, Katherine (Winner of the Baillie Gifford Prize for Non-Fiction): *Super-Infinite: The Transformations of John Donne* – (Faber & Faber, 2022) p.13 Kindle Edition.

chosen perhaps the greatest play by the greatest playwright and begins to show how it focuses on the issue which is central to the human condition, to his own experience and his own philosophy.

Other plays – *Macbeth, Julius Caesar, Othello, Romeo and Juliet* – Lewis contends, depict, in different ways, death as the end. In *Hamlet* we are forced to think, time after time, about *being dead*. Seven examples are cited to give a flavour of this, a flavour that gives the entire play its atmosphere of darkness and uncertainty. In that darkness the characters have lost their way; they need to watch and spy upon each other. The Prince himself gropes for meaning until his famous New Testament echoing line: "There's a special providence in the fall of a sparrow…Since no man has aught of what he leaves, what is't to leave betimes?" It is this recollection (an echo, the source of which, every audience for three hundred years could not have missed) which, I believe, establishes for the first time in the play a sense of calm and purpose in the hero's mind.

Famously, Hamlet hesitates in his task of killing Claudius, the usurping, murderous King of Denmark. The perennial question has, for a long time, been, "Why?" In answer, Lewis says it is not his fear of dying that makes him procrastinate, but his fearfulness of being dead. That state of death is an unknown and introduces uncertainty, unless we either ignore it or give it a value – which is what we do when we limit its paralysing effect by adopting a definite anti-religious or religious stance. Lewis does not believe Shakespeare has given us sufficient data to be certain of this but then gives example after example all of which suggest that the topic is obsessing the Prince. Dissolving flesh, haunting voices, graves, infinite space, shuffling off the mortal coil, bones and skulls, sinners, daring death and danger for an egg-shell, dreams in the sleep of death – all these (and more) constantly remind us of the unknown awaiting us, unless they are banished by faith or its opposite.[6]

At this point Lewis's argument turns towards the similar crucial point he made when speaking about the witches in *Macbeth*. They and the images listed above, we might say, (though Lewis does not link them for us) are there not to tell us more about the character, but about the nature of the world the character lived in – one where the supernatural hovered on every boundary of our fragile existence. Hamlet may for a while lose a high estimation of things (as any of us might under his duress), but Shakespeare, through his poetry, is rather choosing to show us afresh the "great value" of what Hamlet would lose in death, and, seemingly, what we all will, save by the grace of God.

It is now that we can see more clearly perhaps what Lewis was experiencing when he read Morris's *Earthly Paradise*, dealt with earlier on. To Hamlet, the universe is "majestical", and man is "noble in reason…infinite in faculty…in action, how like an angel?" Yet (in the same breath) we are the "quintessence of dust" and vulnerable to every ill-chance and danger. To Morris's Argonauts the world was also sublimely beautiful, so that to leave it is a horror and their quest must be for immortality. As with Morris, so with Shakespeare – albeit at a level beyond Morris's reach: both are depicting Man's essential predicament.

It was a predicament that we know Lewis struggled with. His mother had died before his tenth birthday and while still a teenager he witnessed and suffered the horrors of multiple deaths in trench

---

6 Prof. Stephen Greenblatt brilliantly picks up the uncertainty of Hamlet's belief about death and ghosts in a world where the old Catholic beliefs had been outlawed by the Reformers in his article *Hamlet in Purgatory* (Princeton University Press, 2001)

warfare on the Western Front. By June 1930 he was discussing Owen Barfield's "essay on Death"[7] and even before his conversion, also in 1930, he was conscious that one had to die to many things (e.g. looking to be successful as a writer) in life before death took them anyway.[8] By 1931 he already loved the atmosphere of *Hamlet* which he described as having a prevailing "sense of death." [9] In this same letter to his friend Arthur Greeves, he reveals that it was Morris who taught him how to understand St. Paul's teaching about death. Paul's *Letter to the Romans* is the answer to Morris's failure to find "the true solution" in his story where the whole plot turns on people who set out to find a country where they don't die.[10] The root of the matter, Lewis tells his friend, is *death* and understanding what it means is the key to life. Twenty-five years later Lewis gave to Psyche in *Till We Have Faces* (1956) precisely the understanding which Hamlet (and perhaps his creator) lacked. She feels she has been "made ready for it" (p.83) which Hamlet clearly is not. He *fears* the state which Psyche reaches out towards.

In these two essays Lewis creates a new way of looking at both the plays and their central characters. Rather than *Hamlet* being about doubt or revenge or hesitation or a myriad other things, Lewis makes a strong case for the play being even more universal in its exploration of the human condition and our destiny – something we may not have fully considered. He sees the hero as a man whose mind is fixed "on the frontier of two worlds"; a man incapable of either the rejection or the admission of the supernatural and

---

7 *They Stand Together*, Ed. Walter Hooper (Collins, 1979) p.356

8 Ibid. p.380. In *Till We Have Faces* the god tells Orual "Die before you die." (p.291). Psyche had earlier told Orual that all her life she had had a "kind of longing" to die. (p. 82). When Orual, just days before her death, meets Psyche again, Orual realised she was "being unmade". (p.318)

9 Ibid. p.422

10 Ibid. p.426

HIS LITERARY CRITICISM, HISTORY, THEORY

therefore unable to achieve his aim because he can understand neither himself nor the nature of the universe that produced him. Other motivations for his delay are mere "scaffolding" to the main building, Lewis concludes. And such, it seems to me, is the dilemma of much of humanity through the ages – if not of our own unbelieving one.

Like so much of Lewis's' writing this approach to Shakespeare is both profound while also being, in one sense, profoundly simple. He goes right to the heart of the play (utterly without using critical jargon) and yet at the same time makes this complex drama widely accessible to those who know little of Shakespeare and even less of revenge tragedy. His claim is that we need to have retained unimpaired a "childish response" if we are to be properly grown up.[11] Interestingly, Lewis makes his point here by drawing pictures for us: "night, ghosts, a castle, a lobby...." In his imaginative writing he does the same; he uses universal images which nearly everyone, including children – in the Western tradition – can respond to. Reading aloud the full sentence about "night, ghosts, a castle" gives an idea of how Lewis's awareness of rhythm contributes to the power of his prose. This essay on *Hamlet* is one of his finest.[12]

---

11 Compare: "The chief object of education is to unlearn all the weariness and wickedness of the world and to get back into that state of exhilaration we all instinctively celebrate when we write by preference of children..."G. K. Chesterton, *All Things Considered* (Methuen, 1908) p.59

12 Essays on Donne and Shakespeare may be found in *Selected Literary Essays*

PART TWO

Literary History from the Classical Period to the Sixteenth Century

C. S. LEWIS

THE ALLEGORY OF LOVE

CHAPTER SIX

THE ALLEGORY OF LOVE

Before we progress to Lewis's contribution to Literary History, and to medieval and earlier Renaissance texts, let us allow him to give us some reminders about what we are engaged upon when looking at older literature. In 1944 he wrote the essay, **On the Reading of Old Books**[1] – a practice which he felt was rapidly becoming the exclusive preserve of students of literature and academics, to the detriment of everyone. If that was true of the 1940s then it is immeasurably more true today in an age which is dominated by 'breaking' news, an all-invasive social media presence and a popular culture unaware of anything save itself. A complete absorption in the present does preclude an understanding of the past.

Lewis draws attention to the tendency (still very much present today) to read a modern book *about,* say, Plato, rather than Plato himself – suggesting that the modern book will be longer and duller than the original, as well as not telling you very much about what is *in* Plato. Not only that, but, Lewis believes, the original will be easier to understand than the commentator. This tendency is born partly of humility as we believe the great philosophers to be too difficult for us. A rejoinder to Lewis might be, however, that though certain passages in certain great thinkers are perfectly accessible, finding those without a guide can be daunting and subject to misconception if we know little of the age and context of the writing. Was this not partly why he wrote *A Preface to Paradise Lost*?

---

1 Originally the Introduction to Sister Penelope's translation of St. Athanasius's *The Incarnation of the Word of God* (Geoffrey Bles, 1944)

C.S. LEWIS ON LITERATURE

Lewis saw this kind of approach as especially 'rampant' in theology where he advises us to read either the Scriptures themselves or the great Church Fathers and the theologians (Augustine, Aquinas, Hooker, Butler) whose books have stood the test of time, rather than the complexities of modern theologians. Trying to understand a conversation that began at eight o'clock will be difficult if you join it only at eleven. Today, extended 'real time' conversations on the internet provide an exact parallel: it is often impossible to see the force or humour or relevance or wrongness of a remark or idea if you were not present at the moment when what occasioned it was first spoken. In the case of the latter, one might be seriously misled and accept it as true when others knew that the grounds on which it was made had already been discredited. We might cite some of the novelist Dan Brown's writing as a case in point. Lewis recommends therefore that we should read at least one old book to every three new books. It is the older books that will prevent us from believing too many of our characteristic contemporary errors. New books will merely either tell us truths which we knew in part already, or they will compound the errors which already plague us.

It is worth noticing here that Lewis is talking exclusively in terms of truth and falsehood: books convey either one thing or the other. There is no sense that anything else can be on the menu or that 'my' truth is equal to 'your' contradictory truth or an 'alternative' fact. Unless we can use reason and evidence on which to base our propositions and beliefs about the world, we are indeed doomed.

This commitment to producing criticism which is designed to reveal the essential truth or falsehood of the work under discussion, the veracity, or otherwise, of the concepts and insights the work

HIS LITERARY CRITICISM, HISTORY, THEORY

affords the reader, is immediately apparent in Lewis's first major piece of literary history, *The Allegory of Love*, published in 1936. We have already seen that he conceives of allegory as being the medium which exists not to hide things but to reveal them, a way of bringing to our attention our own inner or spiritual worlds. Before he can talk directly about this however, there is much background to explain about the development of thought in the ancient world. He also explains something of how he came to a monotheistic view himself.

Christians often suppose that fading belief in polytheism – the twilight of the gods – was the consequence of spreading Christian beliefs. But Lewis shows that the process pre-dates this and was well advanced by the time of the Roman poet Statius (AD 45-96) in the first century. Philosophy had already taught such scepticism long before, so we should see monotheism as the maturation of polytheism not as its rival. The "best minds" embraced it while allowing old polytheistic beliefs to be represented as aspects or attributes of God. This is one stage towards allegorising a story.

The next development Lewis shows us is that in the minds of the ancients a profound change took place in terms of how we see ourselves morally, rather than in our thought. For us, the essence of morality appears to reside in the conflict between our duty and what we are inclined to do, or might prefer. That is where we "moderns" all start, says Lewis, as moral beings. The evidence is that if we remove the concept 'temptation' most of what we write or feel about good and evil would simply vanish. But for Aristotle (384-322 BC), the really good person is not subject to temptation. The inner world of warring moral factions (an essential of allegory) was not important.

C.S. LEWIS ON LITERATURE

By the time of the Roman Empire, however, all this has been changed: the moralists were finding, as we do, a conscious difficulty in being good. In Aristotle's *Ethics* the idea of the old hymn, *Fight the good fight with all thy might*,[2] would seem very odd but in the time of Empire the concept is commonplace. Again, this is not the result of Christianity for Seneca (died AD 65) and Epictetus (died AD 135) both express it. Seneca considered conflict to be the *essence* of the moral life. We shall find in this that Lewis has put in place a second aspect of allegory (and of parable), and with it a building block of our moral landscape.

This is a fascinating piece of intellectual history. It has often been thought that the 'Pax Romana' was the best political circumstance for the spread of the Gospel, but here Lewis shows that the whole inner moral world of the West was in the process of change at the time when Paul declared to the Romans, 'All have sinned and fall short of the glory of God'[3]. Monotheism and the 'difficulty in being good' are both captured in those eleven words. But in the pre-Christian world, I think we might claim, the Hebrews were uniquely different. Temptation was part of their mental landscape. Sin – the consciousness of failing to meet the demands of a holy God – was central to Jewish experience both before and after Aristotle. The Fall, the Exodus, the rebukes of the Prophets exist only because Israel fell to temptation, and sinned. Whether this consciousness was a direct result of their monotheism or, more specifically, of belief in a personal, knowable God who speaks and intervenes in human affairs may be debatable.

---

2 Many today would not recognise the concept, let alone the quotation which shows how far we have come since Lewis's day. The fact that this is a metaphor or 'little allegory' for an inner struggle would be a remote idea for most people under middle age – which must impact on how the Church presents the Christian spiritual life to the world.

3 Romans 3:23

HIS LITERARY CRITICISM, HISTORY, THEORY

This new importance given to the world of moral conflict necessarily makes us introspective, invites us "to turn the mind in on itself", to start to explore the world of motive and intention. To do that is to find oneself on the edge of allegory. As the conflict becomes increasingly central so it turns into allegorical poetry. So, true allegory has always found its focus on the inner life; but in a 1956 letter Lewis remarked that from one viewpoint the whole *external* world is an allegory.[4] Poetic allegory similarly makes the *internal* world tangible. By way of summarising the process over time he remarked that on the one hand the gods sank into personification; on the other, a widespread moral revolution forced people to personify their passions. [5]

To crystallise part of the process unforgettably, Lewis chooses to relate one extraordinary moment in this history of turning inward on ourselves: the incident recorded for us in St Augustine's *Confessions* (c. AD 400) when Ambrose is seen to be reading silently; his eyes were moving but no sound came from his lips. A book had suddenly ceased to be a *logos*, audible speech, and had become a succession of mental pictures presented through alphabetic characters. It was a "moment of transition".

A third element in this intellectual and literary history which Lewis encapsulates uniquely well in *The Allegory of Love* is the "creation of the marvellous". He rightly states that most modern readers assume that any creative writer has three worlds to draw upon: the 'actual' world, his religious world and belief system and, thirdly, the world of fantasy and myth. For Shakespeare he suggests these worlds were London and Warwick, the after-life of Heaven

---

    4 *Letters of C. S. Lewis*, Ed. W H Lewis (Geoffrey Bles, 1966) p.273. These and later collections of letters often shed light onLewis's critical opinions.
    5 *The Allegory of Love*, (Oxford University Press, 1936) p.63.

and Hell, and the world of fairies and magic. But these are not to be found at the start of literature when the only marvels were those assumed to be factual. The old gods, after people had ceased believing in them, instead of disappearing altogether, crept back into literature through allegory – not as figures to worship or fear, but cleansed of any taint of reality which would have removed their imaginative power by considerations of practical interest, selfish concern. Thus Lewis draws a contrast between "believed religion" and the realms of the marvellous and fantastic which are *known* to be myth. At first it appears that allegory killed them, but it was so only as a sower buries or "kills" a seed: for like the created beings we are, gods too must die if they are to live.

In this way, Lewis draws us into the "conversation" of Western thought and introduces two ideas which will captivate him for the rest of his life, and which have captivated his readers. First, that it is a law of life, an immutable law, that for a creature to come alive as it is meant to, it must first die. Second, that the mythology of dying and rising gods was a preparation for the moment in history when "myth became fact" in the Crucifixion and Resurrection of Christ in the time of Pontius Pilate, about AD 30.[6] These ideas can be seen in any of Lewis's fiction which has a mythological element to it – most prominently in *Till We Have Faces*. It is well known that he believed myth often contains deep truths about life and that imagination has a key part to play in discovering this. He is not alone. Hilary Mantel in her 2017 Reith lecture said: "Myth is not a falsehood – it is a truth, cast into a symbol and metaphor."

---

6 See for instance, *Myth Became Fact* in *God in the Dock*, Ed. Walter Hooper, (Eerdmans, 1970) p.63 ff. Also *Answers to Questions on Christianity* in *Timeless at Heart*, Ed. Walter Hooper (Fount, 1987) p. 42. There is also a magnificent one-sentence definition of mythology in *Perelandra* (p. 232 Ch.16).

HIS LITERARY CRITICISM, HISTORY, THEORY

Lewis is now ready to begin ("with relief") his exploration of a "much more interesting" period of allegory, the approach to Edmund Spenser's *The Faerie Queene*. He reminds us that the genre was first formed as a result of a change in ethical understanding, and that its first characters were vices and virtues, engaged in moral warfare. This conflict then began to include wider personifications and, in this way, included more of life in its general complexity. Lewis then says that, of necessity, there has to be an imaginary geography for such stories and some making of journeys. But these already existed in the romances so there was a rich field from which to borrow landscapes for imaginary worlds that reflect our inner rather than outer experience.

What Lewis has managed to do here is remarkable. Within a short space he has educated us into an understanding of the origins of not just *The Faerie Queene*, or *The Pilgrim's Progress*, but of subsequent allegorical and fantasy literature, even perhaps Tolkien's. We begin to see that allegory is not just a quaint way of telling a story, but the *only* way certain stories *can* be told. Readers can reflect on to what extent *The Chronicles of Narnia* might be seen in this light. It is not just psychoanalysis that shows us our inner world, but stories do too. As such, even if their first impact is of aesthetic pleasure, or delight, or distraction from the everyday, their profounder meaning can be to help us see more clearly both the causes and consequences of our actions – things which at the point of action are often invisible. The brief, momentary stories in Jesus's parables can be seen as far-reaching in this regard though their 'plot' may be simple.

There is a wonderful image that Lewis uses to describe Spenser's epic poem. He calls it "a great palace" but says that to get into it the only entry is a low door. It sounds a little like the door at the end of

77

The Last Battle, where 'inside' the door is bigger than 'outside' the door and leads to untold marvels. To understand the poem, to be admitted to its secret chambers, we need, he says, a child-like love of the marvellous, a thirst for romantic adventure and a passion for the beautiful. If we can't enjoy it first as a fairy-tale[7] we will not discover that it is so much more. Here again is the principle that was enjoined upon us in reading Shakespeare: that we look to enjoy first those things which all, including children, can enter into: the wild settings, the romance, the courtly or exotic context, the initial imaginative 'feel' (as we might say) of the drama. It is impossible to miss the New Testament parallel, that unless you become as a little child you shall not enter the Kingdom of God. Another law of life seems to be operating here: there is no way forward except through the eye of the needle; the meek shall inherit the earth; he has cast down the mighty from their seats. To enter the new world you must leave behind the baggage of the old – whether it be the world of Spenser, of literary experience generally, or, infinitely more important, the world Christ beckons us towards.

Since Lewis recommended to us the marvels, bogeys and adventures in the poem, there has a been a tremendous growth in the popularity of fantasy literature and film. Lewis and Tolkien were part of the cause of that resurgence. One obvious difference from a hundred years ago is that whereas brighter children of Lewis's generation could cope with the language – and length – of *The Faerie Queene*, rather few today could. A further difference is that

---

7 See *The Allegory of Love*, Chapter 7, "The Faerie Queene". The importance of fairy-tales is also brilliantly captured in G.K. Chesterton's *Fairy Tales* essay: "one idea runs from one end of them to the other...that, if one does the thing forbidden, one imperils all the things provided." *All Things Considered* (Methuen, 1908) p.188ff. Compare *Perelandra* p.83. The point, of course, of the forbidding, the prohibition, is that it makes possible *obedience*. See *Perelandra* p.134 Ch.9.

whereas in Lewis's day very many more people found meaning in their lives from a residuum of Christian belief and morality, today there is widespread search for meaning from alternative sources and some of our foremost thinkers name 'meaning' as the primary need for twenty-first century humanity.[8] Christians should derive some encouragement from this.

Allegory, inevitably, deals with meaning. In Spenser's poem, the philosophical or moral meaning is central, once the marvels have been enjoyed. The poet writes both as Christian and under the influence of Platonism – a thought system which Lewis used for the Narnia stories and believed has much to teach us about appearance and reality.[9] Not only does he re-work Plato's famous myth of the cave in *The Silver Chair*, but he both begins and ends the entire series of Narnia books with Plato's ideas. At the start of the first book he tells us, in the words of Professor Kirke to Peter, that "Nothing is more probable" than "other" invisible worlds, before immediately wondering to himself what on earth they "teach them at these schools". At the end of the last book, the same character, but now elevated as the Lord Digory, having explained that the old Narnia is as different from the real Narnia as a shadow is from the object that casts it, goes on to mutter that the whole idea is in Plato; he then uses exactly the same words as those quoted above. It is as if he expects that the Pevensies should already know this (myth of the cave) as a matter of course.[10] Plato frames *The Chronicles*.

Both Christianity and Platonism posit a meaningful universe and meaningful humanity. In his essay "Edmund Spenser 1552-99",

---

8 E.g. Yuval Noah Harari and Jordan Peterson

9 Plato is also referenced in *Till We Have Faces* e.g. p.292

10 The character is almost certainly a reminiscence of W. T. Kirkpatrick, Lewis's tutor from 1914–1917, his tutor in classical Greek, among other things (notably logic).

Lewis[11] directly and briefly describes how the two thought systems relate. What first unites them is a common belief in a world other than this; an *unbelief* in the idea that 'Nature', the phenomena of time and space, is all there is. For Plato, the difference between them is that of copy and original;[12] for Christians, the difference is between time and eternity, between the imperfect and the unspoiled. But it is also the difference between Man struggling towards the light or out of prison and a God who stoops to lift us out: the Good Shepherd seeking out the lost sheep.

When it comes to describing *The Faerie Queene* itself, Lewis's outline gives us the shape of a deeply Christian poem and advises us to ignore any political or historical allegory we might be looking out for. What is essential to the poem is the philosophical or moral allegory. There are six virtues represented by six knights in six books and each one has to fight against the vice which is opposite to his virtue. In Book I for instance, Holiness has to deal with despair, heresy, pride and error – just the things which will impact any attempt to live a truly religious life. Book II presents us with Temperance who must face lust, avarice and anger. Knights doing battle against the odds was the stuff of the Romances and so a familiar storyline is given profundity and spiritual meaning by the genre. But allegory is not a brain game or Agatha Christie story where we have to puzzle over clues: if, Lewis says, the signification of something after a second look does not seem right or obvious, you are on the wrong track.

---

11 See *Studies in Medieval and Renaissance Literature*, ed. Walter Hooper (Cambridge University Press, 1966) p.144.

12 On Perelandra, Ransom describes having a drink of water as being like meeting "Pleasure itself" (p.38, Ch.3). Later, he confesses he has lived his entire life on Earth among "broken images" and "shadows" (p. 235, Ch.17).

HIS LITERARY CRITICISM, HISTORY, THEORY

Book I then, unsurprisingly is about "Sanctification": how Holiness can restore the lost soul to paradise. The Devil, Father of Lies, has excluded *homo,* or Adam and Eve, but Truth will come to Holiness's aid. This in itself of course held enormous appeal for Lewis as someone who, by his own much later account in *Surprised by Joy*, made his approach to Christianity from an almost entirely intellectual perspective. But there is, he says, another level at work here. The soul is guided by Truth rather than Grace. The fight against the powers of darkness and final defeat of Satan are achieved by Truth because Spenser wrote the poem at a time of "religious doubt and controversy". For the Elizabethans, avoiding error in belief was as important as conquering sin. What *exactly* you believed, mattered: it is Truth that must prevail. They linked errors of understanding with moral instability and therefore with threats to the public good. In the light of all that has happened to society in the past century since Lewis began teaching, perhaps we might be able to say that they were on to something.

Lewis takes us swiftly through the other books of the poem mentioning their central themes. Light and Darkness were the centre of Book I while Health and Sickness are the focus of Book II. The third and fourth books have as their respective subjects, chastity and friendship – two aspects of love. Chastity, it turns out, is "virtuous love" rather than virginity. The three different kinds of love – Eros, Storge, and Philia – are separately classified by Spenser – and readers of Lewis's *The Four Loves* (1960) will be familiar with these already. Spenser also goes as far as to include harmony in the inanimate world as a form of love, something that had already found expression in Plato's *Symposium*. It would find outlet again in the medieval world picture and Lewis's *The Discarded Image* (1964).

Book V, centred on an unattractive and cruel Sir Artegall and justice, is a "stony plateau" but it allows Lewis the chance to explain a past concept of justice that may have eluded us. Political thought between the time of Aristotle and Spenser did not conceive of justice quite as we do. We have egalitarian preconceptions which lead us to assume that fairness is parity: if the cake is the prize and there are two winners it should be divided equally. Earlier thinkers thought the reward should be based on who the two people are. If one is a much better person than the other then the better of the two should get the larger reward. Justice, they believed, is about *proportional* equality in a "fixed social hierarchy" which alone is the way to concord. In the case of this Book, however, it is hard to separate Spenser's depiction of it from his enactment of English policy in Ireland where he was secretary to Lord Grey and complicit in a very bloody massacre and a shameful regime. After all, if your prejudice means that you see some as less human than others, the 'justice' you mete out to them will be especially severe. Lewis felt the historical injustices his countrymen had suffered as keenly as many did, and still do. But if Spenser was a "bad man" in some respects, Lewis reminds us, we should remember that so were Homer (if we judge by his writing), Dante and Milton – in specific areas of behaviour.

It is easy for us to be self-congratulatory about the fact that since the seventeenth and eighteenth centuries, the West has been largely a kind of representative democracy. But vestiges of the old system lasted longer than we think. Three abstract nouns used by Lewis here to describe what justice meant in practice then – liberty, power and honour carefully allocated and graded – describe what was involved in the electoral system in much more recent politics too. In Britain, universal and equal adult suffrage was finally adopted for twenty-one year-olds only in 1948. Prior to that, 'liberty' and the equal power and honour of choosing those who governed lay partly in the hands of the more privileged – by birth or wealth or education. Why our revised understanding of equality took so long to achieve is a question for social and political historians but neither in Britain nor in the USA do we, as 'moderns', have a perfect track record.

The final book, Book VI, comes as a relief. In it we have an examination of 'Courtesy' – but the concept as Spenser understood it, we are told, is no longer part of our scheme of values. It is a combination of humility and charity, in their non-theological senses. It is "the poetry of conduct".[13] Moral effort can take us so far, but there is a grace in behaviour which cannot be learned or taught and which endears to all right-minded people those who have it. Thus, even in this most immeasurable area, we might say (if this is true), it seems we live in an unequal world. It is, on consideration, a Dominical teaching.

Lewis's contention for Spenser is that he has been grossly undervalued by the critics.[14] The final cantos of the poem suggest that, unfinished as it is, there were great beauties still to come. He recognised too that when we reach the "rest of all things, firmly

---

13 When the Lady in Perelandra realises Ransom is not the King of his world, a tone of "deliberate courtesy" enters her dealings with him. (p.75, Ch. 5)

14 In 1962 Graham Hough published *A Preface to The Faerie Queene* (Duckworth) in which he acknowledged that "By far my greatest debt" was to "the writing of Professor C.S. Lewis" about the poem (p.6). In the Index, Lewis has more entries than any other modern critic. In his final chapter Hough writes that Spenser was striving to overcome the split in medieval thinking between amour courtois and the Christian scheme of redemption. He then reminds us that this is the theme of Lewis's *The Allegory of Love* "and there is no need to repeat what he had expounded so brilliantly." (p.231). Hough went on to become Professor of English at Cambridge – so thirty years after publication the impact of the book was still being felt.

stayd / Upon the pillars of Eternity"[15], Change, or Mutability, will be seen as the mode through which Permanence expresses its reality; that the battle between the permanence of the gods and the corruption of Mutability has already been won by the gods. The world may be a battlefield but the outcome is assured. Such a vision, it seems to me, has much in common with those of St. Paul and St. John.

The conclusion to *The Allegory of Love* is a powerful one in which Lewis makes his final appeal to us about the value, beauty and significance of Spenser's great poem. He calls him the "great mediator" between the medieval world and modern poets; the one who prevented too great a renaissance and averted "catastrophe". He was of course a Christian writer and Lewis sees *The Faerie Queene* as a poem even more religious than *Paradise Lost.* No other writer equals him in the creation of the romantic conception of marriage – the basis of our literature of love from Shakespeare to the Victorians. Spenser's work has branches in heaven; it stretches out towards the music of the angels but, at the other extreme, incorporates the horrors of chaos and grotesque satyrs in its range. It covers the complexity of human life but conveys it within the bounds of "chivalrous romance". To read Spenser, says Lewis, is to improve your mental health.

In summary then, Spenser makes inner realities imaginable and uses myth and allegory to show us theological truth. In this way he avoids any sense of devotional writing and anchors his poem in the imaginative world. In doing so, he remains free to draw his own conclusions and share with us his vision of the world.

---

15 *Faerie Queene*, III vi 47

HIS LITERARY CRITICISM, HISTORY, THEORY

In concluding the book this way Lewis has made it impossible for the modern reader today not to draw a parallel with Lewis's own writing of imaginary worlds. In them he uses this same method himself to get past 'watchful dragons'[16] as a way of creating atmospheres and worlds that admit the reader to an (optional) 'religious' experience in the reading but without being explicit. Everyone, not just children, should be able to enjoy a fairy-story and some will find resonances that they respond to almost unwittingly.

Lewis referred to this way of writing as "The Kappa Element in Romance" in a 1940 address in Oxford which he later developed into *On Stories* in 1947.[17] Kappa is the first letter of the Greek word for 'cryptic' or 'hidden from view'. Lewis's experience of reading a wide variety of stories was that the ones he wanted to return to were those that contained "otherness", an atmospheric quality. This is something not immediately apparent to a superficial reader or reading but it can induce almost a "state of being" in the careful reader. In some cases, the mere title can start to evoke it, *The Well at the World's End* by William Morris being a prime example. But Lewis is at pains to say that this is to be aimed at and is not easily achieved.

The essay was published three years before *The Lion, the Witch and the Wardrobe* but the "kappa" idea had been part of his thinking for three decades before that.[18]

---

    16 Walter Hooper, *Past Watchful Dragons*, (Collier Books, 1979) p.ix

    17 For more on this this essay, see Appendix

    18 Michael Ward, *Planet Narnia*, (Oxford University Press, 2008) p.19. There is further consideration of aspects of this approach on pp.127-128

C. S. LEWIS

The Discarded Image

AN INTRODUCTION TO MEDIEVAL AND RENAISSANCE LITERATURE

CAMBRIDGE UNIVERSITY PRESS

CHAPTER SEVEN

THE MEDIEVAL PERIOD

In *The Allegory of Love* Lewis has led us through one aspect of literary history from the Roman Empire as far as Edmund Spenser. We have seen some of the insights of that book. But Lewis was an expert on the literature of the whole medieval period and his lectures on the topic were among his best: enormously popular and eminently memorable.[1] He repeated his "Prolegomena to Medieval and Renaissance Studies" in different forms over a number of decades.[2] These lectures became the basis of *The Discarded Image*, one of his last books. Just as in *The Allegory of Love* he had traced the medieval origins of Courtly Love right through to Spenser, so here he traces the Elizabethan world picture back into the much earlier period. The two ages are not as distinct as scholars had liked to believe – as he had argued in "De Descriptione Temporum": "ages" or "periods" are very imprecise artificial constructs. It is perhaps the most readable of all his work based on his academic lectures. The reviews of it, including those by such distinguished scholars as Helen Gardner and Derek Brewer, were unstinting in their praise, the former writing that no one else could have achieved its form or scope or exactitude. "We are all his pupils" she wrote.[3] Walter Hooper wrote a long summary of it in his *Companion and Guide*, for those who possess that weighty volume, but we shall approach it another way – by combining some ideas from this great book with those of two lectures entitled *Imagination and Thought in the*

---

    1 See Harry Lee Poe, Op. Cit. pp. 122 and 187
    2 *C.S. Lewis: a Companion and Guide*, Ed. Walter Hooper (HarperCollins, 1996) pp.524-5
    3 Ibid. p.548

Middle Ages.[4] Those who want more detail will find *The Discarded Image* an unalloyed delight.

One hallmark of the Middle Ages was its 'bookishness', so before entering into other aspects of that world it is worth referring to one of the last pieces that Lewis wrote, *The Genesis of a Medieval Book*. After dealing with some of the difficulties and sources for two early thirteenth-century texts, Lewis uses the occasion to express his lifelong belief that the personality of an author could not be the proper concern of literary criticism.[5] In it he shows that many medieval works were not authored in the way that Jane Austen is author of *Persuasion*. For many works no one individual can be named as the author rather in the way that (to use Lewis's brilliant analogy) an English cathedral produces a highly satisfying experience even though it is the product of different styles of architecture over many generations. This may not at first seem of much interest to the non-specialist but when we come to examine Lewis's views on originality (part of his contribution to Literary Theory) and why these are important for Christian writers and artists, it will be seen why, in one particular respect, the medieval period appealed to him.

The idea of plagiarism, as we understand it, would have been alien to a medieval author. Anyone studying the texts of the period rapidly finds that the writer has usually drawn heavily on the material of other writers and altered it to suit his purposes or simply because he believed he could do better. Accurate translation, fidelity in use of sources, the very idea of originality, were not things they valued as we do. Rather, the sense is that something

---

4 See *Studies in Medieval and Renaissance Literature*, Ed. Walter Hooper (Cambridge University Press, 1966) pp.41-63

5 We shall see more of this when we consider his contribution to Literary Theory in *The Personal Heresy* (1939)

HIS LITERARY CRITICISM, HISTORY, THEORY

is worth writing and changing *because* it has been written down before. Where and when the process started in any instance may be difficult to trace. Lewis finds the implication of this to be that the personality, even in some cases the identity, of the author cannot be the concern of literary criticism: the poem is what it is and has to be judged according to its merit; the poet is a comparatively shadowy and uncertain figure. Since his stated view was that all criticism should be of books, not their authors[6], this characteristic of the period fitted Lewis's approach very conveniently.

This 'bookishness', the reliance on the written word, is where *The Discarded Image* begins. Lewis notes in his opening chapter that literacy and an awareness of different cultures tend to dissipate savage beliefs. By contrast, medieval beliefs about the universe are *created* by literacy. A poet's belief in 'daemons' for example came from the fact that he had read about them – rather as we believe the accounts of an astronomer or anthropologist in a book or journal. One significant difference however is that, rather like castaways on a desert island, medieval readers were building a culture on the few books not lost to cultural shipwreck and without being able to read their Greek ones. Mostly, their influences came from the Mediterranean area, but there were indigenous and North European influences too and these tend to emerge in Ballads and Romances, something which explains a modern curiosity. Those two genres, Lewis tells us, were atypical of the period and yet their components – knights, dragons, castles, damsels in distress – are today the stuff of popular imagination when most of us envisage the plots of medieval stories. The reason for this is that these genres appealed to the Romantics and that is where Medieval studies began – in the eighteenth and nineteenth centuries. But the real interest of

---

6 *Studies in Medieval and Renaissance Literature*, Ed. Walter Hooper (Cambridge University Press, 1966) p.38

these High Middle Ages was not romantic at all. Arthurian stories, for instance, are a "truancy" from the norm. For medieval man was not an adventurer or even daydreamer, he was someone who liked systems, organised ideas, liked everything to have its logical place and purpose. In literary terms the two greatest examples of this are Aquinas's *Summa Theologica* and Dante's *Divine Comedy*: in each case the ordering of hugely diverse complex material into unity created by passionately logical minds. This picture of an ordered universe is one that Lewis will spend the rest of the book expounding. If we step back for a moment, we might reflect that Lewis himself brought all of life's extraordinary diversity before his own "passionately logical mind" and, in his own way, like the medieval thinkers, presented a coherent and satisfying picture to the Church of the twentieth century as Aquinas had done in the thirteenth.

The library of a medieval scholar could be chosen only from a "chance collection" of ancient Hebrew, Greek, Roman and early Christian texts. Practically all of Plato was missing and Aristotle (later) was available only in Latin via Arabic translators. Athens to Alexandria to Baghdad to Sicily to Paris: that is the route by which such learning reached Europe and thus America and the world. Lewis has no cause at this point to mention that it was the monks at the University of Paris and, centuries earlier, in the scriptoria of the monasteries, (that is, the Church along with Muslim scholars) who made possible this journey in the first place. He does, however, unequivocally say that the medieval picture of the whole cosmos evolved from this: a systematic temperament, great intellectual ability, unwearying patience, and a delight in doing the work. "They tidied up the universe." This is so different from what most people believe about such times as to be almost shocking. If there was a weakness in their approach it could be rightly said that they were too credulous of written authority – not a trait that Lewis by any stretch of the imagination could be accused of, even though he was like them in other respects. My own experience is that only those who have read next to nothing of the literature of this period use the term 'medieval' to describe their state of mind pejoratively rather than any aspect of their technology. Even the riddles and puzzles in their school books would soon silence any such opinion.

The supreme creation of this mindset was the synthesis of all their knowledge which became the Model into which every detail must fit, vast in its scale but readily intelligible: a picture of the whole of God's creation. Lewis's contention is that this gave profound satisfaction to those who lived within it and not only was it a supreme work of art, but the central one of the period. The impact of *The Discarded Image* is such that most readers have agreed with him.

The cosmology of the material universe as the medieval world conceived it is well known: the Earth is at its centre and around it revolve transparent spheres carrying respectively the Moon, Mercury, Venus, the Sun, Mars, Jupiter and Saturn. Beyond them are the stars, all in one sphere, and beyond them the Primum Mobile which powers the movement below it. Last of all (from the earthly point of view) the Empyrean is reached, the beginning of the infinity of heaven. What Aristotle had described as unknown but beyond space and time, the medieval Christianised world made into "the very Heaven" full of pure light and pure love, the abode of God. The whole could hardly be more different from our own secular Models.[7] Lewis's concern, however, and it remains one today, is that the nature of that difference has been utterly misconceived, even by those who should know better. The misconception is that many today imagine that this mistaken view of a seemingly geocentric, anthropocentric universe gave rise to their theology. The implication of course is that the theology too is utterly mistaken – a convenient step for an irreligious generation.

What Lewis then demonstrates is that although medieval theology might be *thought* to imply the high dignity of Earth's central position in the material picture of the Model, their cosmology does not support this view. First, in terms of size: both Aristotle and Ptolemy (who gave the Middle Ages Greek astronomy) are clear that the Earth is of no magnitude whatever and must be regarded merely as a point in the realms of space. The poets and the moralists of the day know this as well as the scholars: the imaginative and emotional impact of the realisation is obvious. We are but a speck in a literally unimaginably large system. Their understanding of human 'dignity' in that respect is not so different from ours. Puffing themselves up was not what their cosmology or their theology could logically give rise to.

The second truth is one Lewis says we need to learn by simple experiment, one he describes evocatively in both in the *Imagination and Thought* lectures and in *The Discarded Image* (*Chapter V: The Heavens*). We should walk alone on a starry night (away from street lights) for thirty minutes with the assumption that the pre-Copernican model is true. You will find yourself looking at

---

[7] In *Perelandra*, Ransom tells Tor the King that the Models of his own universe keep changing, the centre becoming the edge, till no plan is discernible (p.246 Ch.17), and that "darkened minds" see nothing because there are more plans, not fewer or none: "it is all plan". (p.251 Ch.17)

an unimaginably large material world but one that is finite. The Earth being central, you will realise that not merely distance but *height* separates us from the other celestial bodies. We are dwarfed, not to a state of melancholy like Wordsworth and others, but almost to exaltation as we look towards the Primum Mobile, the "largest corporeal thing there is", outside of which is pure Heaven, intellectual light, the Divine Substance. This effect is compounded when we realise that there is a finely graded order throughout: in terms of "size, speed, power and dignity" there is a diminution from the circumference towards our own lowly planet. This is neither machine nor jungle but a beautifully designed building or symphony – a finished work.

When it comes to the "dynamics" of this universe, we are given a salutary reminder. For a medieval philosopher, a flame moved upwards because it wanted to, a stone downwards because it too sought out its home. Our tendency is to smile indulgently at this naivety but Lewis reminds us that this is analogical language and today we do the same. We speak of obeying the 'law' of gravitation but no one imagines there is a literal law of this kind or that the stone decides it had better not break it for whatever reason. But if you fill the universe sub-consciously with "police-courts and traffic regulations" you will have a different mindset from those who fill it with endeavour and longing. In this way Lewis approaches the intersection of medieval cosmology and theology – effectively the theology of Aristotle which they believed was consistent with Christian belief.

The question any generally philosophical mind will ask about this sort of system is, "How does it all get going?" Aristotle's answer was that since the movement of one thing by another cannot be an infinite regression there must be an Unmoved Mover who (or which) moves things by being their 'Final Cause', rather in the way that even the *thought* of food will move a hungry man. So, Lewis explains, for Aristotle, God moves the world by being the *object* of love; not by loving but by being the most desirable object to love. Such an idea necessitates a high degree of rationality being accorded to the moved objects and so every sphere is ruled by an Intelligence which has an unceasing desire to participate in the Divine Nature, to be close to it. The closest approach possible necessitates in turn the circle. As Lewis puts it, their quarry is God; the Intelligences are the huntsmen. Or, if you like, we are his suitors, or the moth hovering as close as it dares to the flame. Such a universe is of course throbbing with life, inhabited by rank after rank of angels, innumerable creatures of pure intellect whose powers of reason compared with ours are as noonday is to dusk. We have to seek out our knowledge by the labour of logical or discursive thought; their minds are entirely intuitive so that difficult ideas in our minds are as immediate and commonplace to them as apples might be to us. By way of illustration Lewis reminds us that even at such a pivotal point as the Annunciation to Mary, she was visited only by Gabriel, an Archangel, who belonged in medieval angelology to the lowest but one class. To put a gloss on that, he could, nevertheless, 'appear' to Mary in a likeness she could fathom, deliver a message in (presumably) Aramaic and then disappear at will. As Lewis says, the fact that we have to think at all about so many (to them obvious) things measures our inferior status. To forget to include them in Christian thinking is to needlessly forego an enrichment of our world.

Life in the heavens, for medieval man, was the reverse of the "silence of those eternal spaces" which famously frightened the

French mathematician, Pascal.[8] All the heavens that his medieval forebears looked at were full of music, a harmony created by the turning of the spheres. They were also full of light. Beyond the apex of the shadow of the Earth, cast by the Sun when it is below us, they believed, was the perpetual light of the Sun. Lastly, the planets themselves were at work upon us. Each influenced humanity in our individual psychology. It was a sort of determinism against which the theologians fought. We might have a bad horoscope, they would say, but by Grace we can get over that just as we can any other trait – a quick temper or greed. Ordinary people accepted planetary influences but equally knew that free will was really free and to listen to astrologers foretelling the future was disapproved.

To give a summary of all that Lewis has to tell us about this aspect of the medieval Model would be to little purpose here, and Walter Hooper has already done so in his *Companion*, mentioned earlier. But one further point must be made. Returning to the experiment of contemplating a pre-Copernican sky at night, we, as moderns, think of ourselves as looking *out*, Lewis writes. We look out from somewhere warm and lit at an indifferent universe – cold, dark and somehow desolate. For the medieval contemplator, it was different. They looked *in*,[9] and it was for them *the Earth* which was outside the city wall, placed as it were, around the orbit of the Moon and so excluding us. For a moment at night, we are told, the gates would open for them and they could see a glimpse of the revelry and dancing going on inside, like animals staring at the camp fires they dare not approach.

---

8   The final pages of *Perelandra* brilliantly illustrate this where Ransom is told that there is no "eternal silence" in the celestial places to which he cannot go.
9   Compare Ransom's feeling in *Perelandra* (p.23 Ch.2) as he looks from Earth up at the night sky and realises that "*in there*" (Lewis's italics) were friends who would welcome his return to Malacandra.

Given that every picture or Model we create of the universe is necessarily an analogy, it may be instructive to reflect that the picture we hold in our heads can either diminish or enhance our spiritual life. The picture that Lewis re-creates for us here seems to me to be an enrichment. We can see ourselves once more as creatures, not accidents, part of a magnificent creation of unimaginable complexity and overwhelming beauty. At the same time we are reminded that ours is a "silent planet" in comparison with untold other worlds; that the joys and beauties we can know here are as nothing in comparison with what awaits as we go "further up and further in" towards the centre of the festival.

Such a picture explains much of Medieval culture, Lewis says. Instead of the people of that age liking high ceremony and therefore imagining heaven in that way, as a modern commentator might say, the age saw it the other way round. Their church and social hierarchies were known to be pale reproductions of the celestial realities. Every pageant and ceremonious ritual was an attempt to copy how the universe worked. They liked to hear and to tell the story, with the result that poems and buildings became "verbalised or petrified cosmology". It was the desire of the outsider to join the life of the city so far as he could.

Lewis chooses to end both his *Imagination and Thought* lectures and his book with two provisos. The first is to remind us that he has invited us to consider this picture of the medieval cosmos as a work of art, rather than a statement of fact. It was perhaps, he says, the greatest the Middle Ages produced, unequalled in splendour and coherence. Not a fantasy, they intended it to make sense of all the known facts and it pretty much did that.

HIS LITERARY CRITICISM, HISTORY, THEORY

The second proviso is to draw our attention to the way the changes to our current Model of things has come about. It was not solely the intrusion of new inconvenient facts in astronomy and biology that caused the alterations. Nor was it the fact that anything we can imagine is now further from the truth than the conclusions of mathematics about our universe – which cannot be imagined in the sense of telling us what the universe is like. Rather, it is that when a change in the human mind produces "sufficient disrelish" of the old ways of thinking and desire for a new one is strong enough, new facts, different phenomena, seem very helpfully to appear. They are not illusions, but Nature has a wide variety of things on offer from which we tend to choose those that support our presuppositions.

We know, Lewis concludes, that every age is influenced by how it sees the world, by the Model that predominates, but it's a two-way street: the Model itself is created in part by what people are already thinking. Ideas about Evolution long precede Darwin. We do not move simply from error to truth; each Model is a statement of an age's psychology as much as of its factual knowledge. By way of analogy, the evidence that appears in a court of law is dependent on the nature of the examination. The facts may not be falsified but the ones that are brought to light are the ones that will create a pattern for the judge and jury. Posterity will judge our Models as we judge those of earlier ages.

Characteristically, Lewis has given us not just a brilliant, compelling, absorbing glimpse of the medieval Christian world but has, almost in the same breath, drawn attention once more to the limitations of our own error-strewn and secular society.

CHAPTER EIGHT

THE SIXTEENTH CENTURY

Professor Fleming of Princeton University calls Lewis's volume in The Oxford History of English Literature, *(English Literature in the Sixteenth Century excluding Drama)* "The greatest single monument to Lewis's astonishing literary erudition."[1] Many others also thought this his best work. It took him a full ten years to complete his expansion of the original 1944 Clark lectures. He was pioneering in establishing the realisation that literary developments in Europe between 1300 and 1700 were not characterised by two separate periods, the Middle Ages and the Renaissance, but that the whole period was understood more clearly to be a series of gradual developments rather than a time of revolutionary change. But at the time it was a controversial contribution to intellectual history. Had the term 'Renaissance' continued to mean simply a revival of learning especially with regard to Greek and Latin Lewis tells us he would have used it. As it was, however, the term's meaning had widened so much that it had become "an imaginary entity" – one used to describe what the speaker liked about the period. It was a useless descriptor and one that, by implication, denied the Middle Ages the brilliance Lewis manages to convey to us elsewhere.

Lewis was also concerned to counter the view that humanism played a large part in the flowering of literary genius and 'science' in the later part of the period. He believed the humanists despised the past outside their favoured periods, were "narrowly ethical" and set a fashion for aping the past style of a few chosen texts. He also believed that the loss of the Medieval sense of hierarchy in the universe may have allowed a kind of freedom but that it also

---

1 *The Cambridge Companion* p. 23

brought a negative determinism which undermined humanity's right conception of the roles of Creator and creature. A further misconception Lewis sought to correct was the misunderstanding of the word 'Puritan' – something we have seen him touch on when writing about Donne. A final point at this stage is worth making by way of summary: it is usual to think of this period as a time of liberation and adventure – both intellectual and geographical. Indeed it was, but, we are reminded, there were also growing constraints on liberty: Calvinism on freedom of the will, new theories of sovereignty on political freedoms, and Humanism on style and emotions. Perhaps no age flows entirely in one direction.

This is a book of nearly 700 pages and every page reveals painstaking scholarship expressed in the clearest and most compelling prose. I shall pick out from it a few ideas which general readers today, without any particular knowledge of the period, are likely to find of interest.

Lewis divides the century in two in terms of the style of its authors. He calls them either "drab" or "golden". This is doubtless a deliberate simplification but the number of mediocre writers whose use of imagery and sound is uninspired, heavy-handed and ploddingly earnest is so prolific that they need to be separated from the golden-tongued if most readers are to make headway in the period. It was in the last quarter-century that the colour and life suddenly, unpredictably, returned: Sydney, Spenser, Shakespeare, Hooker are the names Lewis especially picks out and nothing in the history of the period could have enabled even the keenest eye to predict this flowering that was to last a hundred years. To those who know of this flowering, Lewis suggests, the very sense of the words *England* and *Aristocracy* has been given a new richness.

HIS LITERARY CRITICISM, HISTORY, THEORY

Rather than analysing the causation of this literary phenomenon – *why* there should be so many men of genius – Lewis sketches the intellectual and imaginative background to the period. He accepts, of course, that "many movements of thought" would not have been possible without the rediscovery of Greek, but asserts that the flowering of English literature in this period is not the result of it. Humanism, for which the study of Greek was of central importance, had neither the power nor the wish to encourage the sort of writing that emerged. Lewis thus puts that powerful intellectual movement in its place and provocatively associates the *renascentia* of Renaissance Humanism with "new ignorance" in his chapter heading. He justifies this by explaining that the Humanists in particular had an aversion to the chivalric romances and scholastic philosophy of the Middle Ages – so much so in fact that important books were burned and a sort of "Philistinism" resulted. So the New Learning created a New Ignorance. Some have reservations about this of course[2] and they would say that Lewis's love of the Medieval world led him to overstate the case against those who deplored the earlier age. It's a truly academic argument and we can move on from it.

What is more useful to the non-specialist reader is the light Lewis sheds on the new astronomy – he is referring to the revolutionary theory published by Copernicus in 1543, that the Earth revolved around the Sun. Because it was only a surprising *theory* (verification came later with Kepler and Galileo) and it was not widely known or accepted, we should not imagine that it had anything like the impact of Darwin upon the Victorians or Freud on the twentieth century. Moreover, the Earth was known to be a sphere, to be infinitesimally small and to be "the worst and deadest part of the universe" in Montaigne's words. So mankind's "dignity"

---

2 E.g. Dennis Danielson in *The Cambridge Companion*, p. 47

was not impaired. As we know from *The Discarded Image*, previous ages already considered Earth to be at the rim, furthest from the intellectual and spiritual centre of everything. Any loitering idea therefore that men of genius arose in such great numbers because they had thrown off the shackles of Medieval faith and thought is put out of court.

One further undeception that Lewis is concerned to make here is the dismantling of the way we impose modern categories on past groups of practitioners. For most of us, magic and astrology belong together as sub-rational beliefs, as superstition. In the sixteenth century, however, these two groups were in opposition to each other and clearly distinguished.[3] The magician was claiming extraordinary powers over nature, while the astrologer sought to demonstrate how little power we have when it comes to the natural world. Humanity, he believed, was at the mercy of the constellations, the plaything of planetary influence. His counterpart today would be a scientific determinist who might substitute genes for planets whereas 'magician' connotes merely the idea of 'entertainer' since we no longer believe in the power of magic, only of illusion. The lessons to be learned are obvious enough but have not always been attended to. The first is that the Church has had to contend for freedom of the will in centuries long before our own mapped the human genome or attributed so much human behaviour to genetic influences. Secondly, unless we understand properly what the people of a previous age were being presented with in terms of assaults upon their faith, we will not react appropriately to their responses. Today, a witch is most often seen by the world as a misguided but harmless old woman and so it is easy to laugh at her midnight mutterings. When she was thought to be in league with

---

[3] Lewis cites the Italian philosopher, Pico della Mirandola (1463-94), who attacked astrology but defended magic.

HIS LITERARY CRITICISM, HISTORY, THEORY

Lucifer and capable of harming your baby, or ruining your crops, you might well have reacted differently.

The section of the opening chapter which deals with the great voyages of discovery to the 'New World' will provide new light for most readers on how these affected the imaginative writing and philosophical thought of the period. Not surprisingly, the new awareness of geography was more exciting to most than the new astronomy. A direct route to the east, a means of stealing a march on Venetians and Turks, would put money, perhaps untold wealth, in the pockets of merchants and investors. The old teaching that the earth was a sphere meant that the sufficiently brave could sail west to find the east. For those attempting or investing in the dream we need to remember that the fact of America was a huge disappointment – one of the greatest in Europe's history, Lewis tells us. Its enormous land mass was not the imagined series of islands beyond which Cathay could be reached via the 'South Sea' (Pacific) on their far side. Denied Cathay, the Spanish were reduced to more local exploitation of mineral wealth. The English, beaten to it as it were, could merely colonize the coast – mostly with misfits and criminals in a "social sewerage system". It was a second-best option which meant they were often uncomprehending of what they found, where the water in Virginia smelt so sweet that it seemed to come from "some delicate garden" and where the indigenous people were as "civil as any in Europe". It seemed "the golden age" had been rediscovered. But Protestant missionary endeavour seems entirely missing from the earliest records.

Later writers like Charles Kingsley invested the voyages with romantic charm or idealistic Imperialism, but to those who made the original voyages the places often had little appeal. Their intent was always to discover peoples and cities. "Plains without palaces" did not yet capture their imagination in the way we have seen began to develop in the eighteenth century. Such vast expanses of wild nature were still, by long experience, usually more threat than opportunity.

In the light of the current debate about the ethics of Empire and the sins of colonization, Lewis's view on the issue is especially interesting. It is not an area he often touches on – there was no need. But here he succinctly, in a single sentence, conveys a view. It was, he says with irony, to be a long time, a period of extensive training, before the best consciences in Europe found themselves able to accept, or acquiesce in, an "untroubled" view of nineteenth century imperialism. Go back to Burke, or Johnson or Montaigne's *Essays* and you will find a sense of shame about European exploitation in America. If Lewis is right in this, then the best Christian minds in sixteenth century Europe knew intuitively, or by teaching, that the subjection, exploitation or even enslavement of other peoples was profoundly wrong. His insight here is useful in modestly defending the history of the Church: (for most of its first millennia and a half) by stating that its history (though not that of the nations) is more one of emancipation of subjugated peoples than enslavement of them. It is not a fact that we hear frequently expressed today for the horrors of the slave trade have, understandably, eclipsed it in modern minds – but Christians should be aware of such facts and thus capable of informing those conscious only of media-led and inaccurate views.

In literary terms, the disappointments of the voyages meant that what we perceive to be their wonder was seldom the focus of imaginative writing at the time. Lewis mentions "casual references" in four authors (More, Spenser, Shakespeare, Donne) but found that imaginations at the time were centred still on the ancient world, and on English legend or history. It is interesting that he does not mention in this context Shakespeare's late play, *The Tempest*, which is surely more than a "casual" reference to the excitement and wonder generated by fabulous stories of sailors crossing the Atlantic. The play is, however, mentioned when Lewis comes to examine the imaginative and philosophical legacy of the voyages of discovery.

That legacy was partly to create, partly to impress on us, the imagined concept of uncivilised or 'savage' Man. Today, of course, the word is no longer in acceptable use but for Lewis's generation it was a standardised term denoting those living where the culture was illiterate, 'natural' and beyond the influence of the great civilisations. Christians, Stoics and poets had variously envisaged such a person in the past – Adam, the state of Nature, or the Golden Age – but some who returned from America had tales that suggested a present reality. Such tales gave rise to a double-edged myth. One side of this produced the good 'Salvage' in the *Faerie Queene*, also the point in *The Tempest* where Gonzalo describes the perfect commonwealth, the 'reign of God' in Pope's *Essay on Man*, and, for the Marxists, their classless primeval society. The other side produced a less than human, brutish figure: Caliban in *The Tempest*, Thomas Hobbes's depiction of Man in his natural state and our own popular conception of the 'Cave Man'.

Thus it was, we might go on to say (though Lewis does not), that the idea of society vitiated by Original Sin – a doctrine promulgated through Christendom – was confronted with an alternative understanding of Man's fundamental nature. Are we more like Rousseau's 'noble savage' but corrupted by civilization, or are we now more truly characterised by 'total depravity' which since Augustine had become a central teaching of the Church? Are we now (post-Fall) fundamentally good or fundamentally bad? It seems that the debate, even if it existed before, took on a new topicality as a result of the new geography.

Mention has already been made of Lewis's concerns about the misunderstanding (as he saw it) of the role of the Humanists and Puritans in sixteenth-century Europe. We have not, however, seen the strength of his feeling about this or how this might have an impact on our understanding of the world today. The simplest approach to this is to flag up the fact that, as with previous groupings, we must not apply current usages of the words to the world of 400 years ago and earlier. To do so would be to misunderstand entirely not only what was happening then but to create a rod for our own backs. Both parties were to change the face of Europe and, in many cases, the two parties were one. Today, *puritanism* in the moral sense is seen to be *asceticism*, the stance of an abstainer in one or more areas. Humanism, Lewis suggests, for his generation too, meant pretty well the opposite of puritanism. Today we would have to add that it describes a well-meaning secularity, perhaps based on a purely scientific approach to philosophy.

For the Elizabethans, puritanism was first of all about church organisation; a Puritan was someone who disapproved of episcopal governance of the Church of England and likely to argue for a Geneva-style state – as under Calvin. But there was a gradation of belief, many wanting to remain within the Establishment. But strongly emphatic doctrines linked them together, namely: justification by faith, the centrality of preaching as the main means of grace and a disbelief that Scripture accorded the bishops of the day their authority. It is a serious historical error with repercussions today to imagine that Puritans were not Humanists because to place the two groups in opposition (rather than recognising the overlap) once more discredits the Church. It makes the Puritans into killjoys and by implication into obscurantists – by virtue of the fact that the sixteenth-century Humanists are the group known today, as then, to be central to the provision of Greek and (the better) Latin texts, thereby opening up a new world of study. In fact, Lewis will argue, the obscurantists were, in some respects, the Humanists while the Puritans were the forward-looking intellectuals who tended to be young and fashionable. They were more averse to bishops than they were to beer. The limitation of the humanist approach was that it made its focus the *style* of the Latin authors rather than what they said; it created a vogue for 'classical' or 'correct' Latin while at the same time dismissing the medieval world of chivalry, romance and scholastic philosophy.⁴

Put in this way, it is perhaps evident why Lewis felt these misconceptions were important to reveal, not just for historical and literary purposes, but for his own age more generally. Even before Darwin and right up into Lewis's own lifetime, Christianity had been accused (as it is today) of the two traits that the sixteenth century Puritan was also deemed to have manifested: a 'Thou shalt not' attitude towards the pleasures of life and a reluctance to take on board the intellectual and scientific discoveries of its own age. (By way of example, in 1947 Lewis had published *Miracles*, a book that some atheist Oxford academics had sought to ridicule for its belief in the supernatural, even while not being able to refute its arguments.⁵) If the true nature of sixteenth century thought was to be understood, and intellectual history properly preserved, then Lewis needed to spell it out. If it also removed one of the stumbling-blocks to 'modern' belief by its saving re-alignment of

---

4 "Edmund Spenser, 1552-99." C.S. Lewis, *Studies in Medieval and Rennaisance Literature*, (Cambridge University Press, 1966), pp.121-145.

5 See A.L. Rowse, *Glimpses of the Great* (Methuen, 1985), p. 206

Church History from the pronounced anti-religious bias of the mid-twentieth century, that would be a powerful additional incentive for making this opening chapter of a seminal work as striking and inescapable as possible. Anyone contributing to the debate simply could not ignore it if they wished to hold a view on the subject.

Lewis's stated aim as literary historian was, in large part, to enable students and his wider public to get as close as possible to the experience of living in the period under discussion. What we all want to know, he suggests, in this instance, is to experience what it would feel like to *be* one of those early Protestants. The combination of intense imaginative powers, the skills of a novelist and brilliant erudition and scholarship enabled him to do this as few, if any others, have done. We might expect, therefore, that he would begin to describe the experience in literary terms – that it was emphatically not like that of 'puritans' in nineteenth-century fiction such as Dickens's Mrs Clennam in *Little Dorrit* who tried to expiate her sins by choosing life-long gloom as her norm. Indeed, an early Protestant would have seen such expiation as papistical, a corrupt practice of the old Religion. The recovery or development of Pauline theology meant that any such attempt was known to be fruitless, impossible. Experientially, a moment of catastrophic change, of realisation, lay behind this – as strong, Lewis suggests, as waking "from nightmare into ecstasy"; the equivalent of the sudden acceptance of the previously spurned lover: a moment of astonishing joy. And, Lewis continues, the whole reality has come to you free, a gift of overwhelming grace initiated by God and untarnished by time: a 'forever' gift. The old doctrine of 'works' now moves into what we do as a *result* of the gift, not because we think they can earn us the reward. The belief in this realisation, the recipient's 'faith' creates a "buoyant humility" and from this, sprang the original doctrines of Protestantism. The associations of gloom or sourness or severity that now cling to *puritan* as a word are therefore completely wide of the mark when thinking of their first appearance. Even their enemies, Lewis claims, did not charge them with this.[6] It would be quite wrong to infer from this, however, that they took sin lightly. Adultery and fornication were seen as deadly sin, but so were they seen by the Roman church which was even stricter – evidenced by its exaltation of virginity rather than marriage as the highest state.

There are many passages woven into this long book which simply on their own stand out as descriptions, even evocations, of a powerfully affecting kind, quite apart from whether the reader is familiar with the period and books that Lewis has as subject. This section, so close to Lewis's own heart, is undoubtedly one of them.

As we move towards Lewis's writing on the most famous of all books, the Authorised Version of the Bible, it is important that we look at some of Lewis's comments about the role of William Tyndale (1494-1536) who was, in the opinion of many scholars, our greatest single translator of Scripture and the source for ninety per cent of the New Testament translation in the AV.[7] He was a leading light in the Reformation and the first to translate the Hebrew and Greek Scriptures into English.

For Tyndale, the purpose of the 'gospel' was, as Lewis describes his view – rather alarmingly perhaps – to save the world from *morality*. The expression commands attention. Tyndale, he

---

6 It is true, however, that fun was poked at those who most evidently were hypocritical in their profession of the new faith – certainly by the 1600s. The tormenting of Malvolio in Shakespeare's *Twelfth Night* by Feste and Sir Toby Belch is a case in point. Sir Toby knows, interestingly, that Malvolio isn't a 'real' puritan.

7 See Manifold Greatness, *The Making of the King James Bible* (Bodleian Library, 2011) p.28

suggests, believed in psychological determinism when it came to considering the natural human condition. Human nature, 'fallen' as it is, cannot be changed merely by moral effort.[8] Making 'charity' into a duty is, Lewis says, exactly what the early Protestants intended to do away with. Obedience to moral rules produces pride when what is required instead is a new sort of creature – one that is not seeking its own profit. And here, perhaps, some Christians today may be brought up short by Tyndale's reminder that human nature knows nothing of disinterestedness. It is, as Lewis puts it, as hedonistic to seek a place in heaven for one's own advantage as it is to seek worldly wealth. Yet it is that disinterestedness, that lack of selfish motives, which the moral law demands. We are thus in a position of despair – until the 'rain' of the gospel replaces the 'thunder' of the law. At that point, Tyndale tells us, we become free, for the only truly free will in existence can conjoin with our own, as Supernature supplants Nature by God's grace bestowed by the gift of faith. In this way, duty has been turned into love. Just as God has overcome us, his enemies, with love, so we in turn find power to love even our enemies.

Tyndale speaks of this transformation as producing in the receiver laughter and gladness to the very "bottom of his hart" – a far cry from the imagined severity or even prudishness the Puritans are frequently accused of today. And here Lewis finds it impossible to forbear from a comment on how "tragically narrow is the boundary" between this great reformer and those who opposed him: what *he* meant by faith means so nearly what *they* meant by charity: not the freedom to dispense with 'works' but the deeply sensed desire to do such 'works' – to fulfil the moral law and thus

---

8 In *Till We Have Faces*, Orual realises in the penultimate chapter that she could no more mend her soul by effort than she could her (ugly) face. (p.293)

HIS LITERARY CRITICISM, HISTORY, THEORY

be free of its 'fretting' demands.

Lewis's intention when writing about the Church and its beliefs was always to try to present 'mere' Christianity, a picture of a shared faith that was universal. To do anything which might further divide believers was to him of the utmost seriousness[9], a means of causing "little ones to stumble". Here is one reason for that: he saw that the greatest divide in the history of Christendom was, in part, based on misunderstanding as well as self-seeking and sheer worldliness. More and Tyndale were vociferously, and in the end violently, opposed and yet the ends they sought were not distant from each other and many of their intellectual assumptions were the same. Ironically, they both suffered a similar martyr's fate for the differing doctrinal positions they held.

This stance that Lewis takes becomes apparent again when he speaks of Tyndale as a translator. He picks out the word *ekklesia* which Tyndale contentiously translates as *congregation*, *presbuteros* which he translates as *elder* and *charis* which is translated as *favour*. Lewis makes the point (seldom made) that as Tyndale looked at the Church of his day with all its accretions of hierarchy, buildings, inquisitions and wealth it would have been, in his view, misleading to translate St. Paul's word in such a way as to evoke that institution. Sir Thomas More, however, equally felt that the Church he knew was, mystically, the same body that St. Paul had addressed 1500 years earlier; *ekklesia,* therefore, could *only* be translated as *Church.* To do otherwise was to undermine the foundations. So it is that every translation is an (often unrealised) implicit commentary. All translations begin from a premiss that will direct the outcome. In addition, it is difficult for translators to be fully independent.

---

9 See W. Hooper's recollections in his Preface to Lewis's *Christian Reflections* (Geoffrey Bles, 1967) p. xi

Genius though he was, Tyndale was in debt to Erasmus, to Luther and to the Vulgate; he shared too, with Luther, the conception that whatever the translation was it should be within the plough-boy's reach.

It has already been said that Tyndale was largely responsible for the text of the New Testament in this new 1611 Authorised Version. Lewis concurs with this, adding Coverdale's name (1488-1569) and the versions produced in Geneva in 1560 and Rheims in 1610. What is less straightforward is the matter of trying to assess the literary value and influence of this great work, largely the product of sixteenth-century scholars.

Lewis finds that the literary *value* of the translation depends not only almost entirely on the original material for its matter, tropes and images but on its "liturgical associations". Moreover, trying to isolate the work of the last translator from the host of previous ones is very difficult. The rhythms of the AV do not provide an answer about its value either as he very wittily shows by substituting the words *cocktail, soup* and *small, cold pie* for the famous triplet of *earthquake, fire* and *still small voice* in I Kings xix.12 – the story of Elijah's encounter with God on Mount Horeb. The rhythm of the new sentence is the same but the impact of it is ludicrously different. Lewis boldly suggests instead that the importance some critics have attached to the *style* of the AV is a substitute for the fact that their belief systems disallow much value being attached to its *content*. In the simplest possible terms, we might say, it is *what happens* in the Bible that has determined its value, not its style.

Equally interesting is Lewis's assessment of its literary *influence*. As elsewhere, Lewis reminds us that a conscious influence is very different from, and usually much less effective than, an unconscious influence and that the Bible's is mostly of the former kind. This is especially true in the nineteenth and early twentieth centuries. Quotation and parody of the text, its use in providing solemnity, its sanctity, its archaisms, precisely because they were recognised for what they were, stand out from their context and never "penetrated into the blood-stream" of the literature. The familiar phrases of the Bible are more like plums set into a cake than water mixed with wine. In this way Lewis sets on its head the commonplace idea that the AV has had immeasurable influence on subsequent writing. Rather, as he makes clear in his essay on John Bunyan, much of the writing would have been what it is, without the publication of the Authorised Version.

Today, the "anonymous and corporate work", the *Book of Common Prayer* of 1549, is even less known than the 1611 Bible but for four hundred years was familiar to churchgoers throughout England. Its chief author was Thomas Cranmer, Archbishop of Canterbury, who famously supported Henry VIII in his assumption of sovereignty over the Church in England and who was burnt at the stake by the Catholic Mary Tudor. For those familiar with the language of the BCP Lewis has interesting insights as to how its unmistakeable phrasing came about in terms of sources and translations of earlier Latin texts; how its coupling of near-synonyms – such as "sins and wickednesses" for instance – creates the rhythms that direct our responses and which a literal translation of the Latin *peccata* would have lacked. Moreover, out of the conflict, he suggests, between the "Drabness" of that age of earnestness and the ripe artistry of its originals, "perfection springs". At its best, Lewis says, it shines a light so bright that only the New Testament itself surpasses it.

PART THREE

LITERARY THEORY

The Personal Heresy

a contro-versy

C. S. Lewis

E. M. W. Tillyard

CHAPTER NINE

CHRISTIANITY AND LITERATURE

Theorising about literature goes back at least to Aristotle. What literature is for and how it works on the reader was a continuing interest for Lewis who, in his first brief university role taught philosophy. In all, he wrote seven books entirely or partly dedicated to literary theory as well as a number of essays and addresses. But Lewis founded no new 'school' of theorists precisely because he was in the line of an ancient tradition. He often went right to the heart of what were seen by others as critical issues without adopting the approach of any one school of thought — as we saw in his writing on *Hamlet*. Theoretical concerns about gender, race, nationality, politics and so on which have subsequently occupied critics and readers were not exercising his generation in the way they did for those who came later. For fifty years (from the 1950s) theory took the first place ahead of reading the original works — but the tide has turned.[1]

To what extent Lewis's viewpoint as a critic derived from his Christian beliefs is an interesting and fundamental question, one that can be answered in part by turning to his early essay, *Christianity and Literature*. It began life as a talk to a religious society in Oxford and was published in 1939 in his second book of literary criticism, *Rehabilitations and other Essays*. The essay contains valuable insights as to how a Christian might approach literature

---

1 See Alastair Fowler's view in Harry Lee Poe, op.cit. p.114. Elsewhere D. O. Ross makes the interesting point that such criticism turns away from the books to theory rather in the way that Lewis saw that Renaissance Humanism became seduced by its own precepts. *(C. S. Lewis's lost Aeneid*, ed. A. T. Reyes, (Yale University Press, 2011) p. xxiii

of all kinds. Much later he softened the tone of these early views but did not greatly alter them. They find further expression in his essays *Bulverism* and *Membership* and also much later in the books *An Experiment in Criticism* and *Letters to Malcolm*, his last book.

Lewis tells his audience that he has made the discovery that there is an incompatibility between the ideas prevalent in modern criticism and those of the New Testament. He found that whereas critics are looking for creativity[2] and spontaneity coming from great authors deemed to be innovative and pioneering, the model of behaviour in the New Testament is based on imitation and reflection. Bad writing in today's world is, by contrast with the good, seen to flow from conforming to rules, conventionality. There is therefore a "repugnance" in atmosphere between these two ways of looking at human endeavour. Lewis refutes the claim that Our Lord was especially a poet or profoundly literary. He was as much philosopher as poet; Lewis cites the parable of the Unjust Judge (who is unlike God both imaginatively and emotionally) as an example of the sort of method the philosopher Socrates used rather than how a poet thinks or teaches. Jesus's tendency to use *argumenta ad homines*, which is the practice of using your accuser's own beliefs and arguments against them, and the *a fortiori* approach which is arguing from an accepted conclusion to an even more evident one, are further citations of Jesus's philosophic mindset when occasion called.

Originality, Lewis seeks to argue, is, in the Bible's view, God's prerogative not ours. Our happiness, our duty, is to be found in working like a mirror to reflect the nature of God. Life, in

---

2 Lewis pokes fun at the idea that we can be genuinely "creative" in *Perelandra* where he has the Green Lady burst into uncontrolled laughter when she finally realises what Weston, the Un-Man, means when he uses the word. (p.150 Ch.10)

HIS LITERARY CRITICISM, HISTORY, THEORY

Christian terms, is rightly lived conscious of the derivative status of our minds and gifts, not their originality. Our aim should be to acquire a "fragrance" that is borrowed, or to change the metaphor, to be mirrors that reflect a face that is not our own. The alternative is pride – not just coming before a fall but which is a fall in itself – our attention falling from better to worse, from God to oneself. When applied to writing 'literature' as opposed to criticism, this theory means that an author is the partial embodiment of wisdom and beauty not their own. Such a view has an affinity with Homer's Muse, with Plato's doctrine of Forms, Aristotle's *mimesis* and with Augustine. It is in opposition to the idea of literature as self-expression.

Lewis's view therefore has the longest possible tradition behind it but remains in sharp distinction from practically everything our own generation (and his) has learned to assume about artistic genius and 'creativity'. Today, 'self-expression' is taken almost invariably as the norm for all writing, and for daily behaviour. The four theories of poetry Lewis cites are all from the ancient world. Subsequent theories emphasised the self as the source of genius, which suggests a gradual diminution of the sense of God being the original Creator of all. As people lose their sense of being 'fearfully and wonderfully made' they find alternative ways of asserting their identity – with predictable social consequences.

Some may think Lewis too extreme here in thinking the New Testament allows no room for creativeness. But elsewhere Lewis remarked, by way of clarification, that it was the focus on *trying* to be original that was mistaken. Originality would emerge if the writer was focused on something else. Thus, being 'original' is a quality that both believer and unbeliever can share, but with one fundamental difference: the unbeliever can take his own experience and value it merely because it is his own. The believer should (Lewis says 'will') deal with it as the point from which a perception "universally profitable" was granted to him. In this way, though Augustine and Rousseau each give us their *Confessions*, for Rousseau his individuality is a sort of absolute, while for Augustine it is a place too narrow for God: "it is in ruins – oh rebuild it" he pleads.

In the twenty-first century it may genuinely be difficult to negate personality in the way Lewis seems to suggest that authors should. It is not wrong to ask whether we should think of ourselves as mere conduits or rather as sparks of divine fire whom God has entrusted with a (now) fragmented creativity, partly reflective of his Being. If our insights are valuable because they are a unique part of the Truth, perhaps this would constitute a middle way between the two alternatives Lewis presents us with.

Lewis now has a concluding point to make. It is one that we have seen him make in later essays when he felt the results of it most keenly. It is that Christians will find that they understand the study of literature to be a slightly less serious affair than their cultured but pagan friends who may tend to turn aesthetic experience into a kind of religion. A religion in which, being highly educated, such a person is elevated above the masses who read for mere enjoyment. By contrast, Christians know that the saving of a single soul outweighs the literatures of the world and that the poor, who have less opportunity to read, are likely to be our moral superiors. If we are seen to take the shallow view that we can merely play and be amused to the glory of God, it should not be thought that good Christian writing cannot reach the sublime upon the greatest of all themes. For it is not literature which is the greatest thing, but that towards which great literature points, whether it be a ballad of border-raids or an epic about the loss of Paradise. Valuing literature for its own sake, says Lewis, is a "solemn vacuity".

Amongst the 'highly cultured' we might well still say today that in some cases the arts do become a sort of religion to those beyond the confines of the faith. One could argue that it cannot be otherwise. If there is no salvation in God, if there is no God, then there is no soul to save eternally anyway; so literature may 'save' some in temporal terms by its cultural and humanising influence; by its broadening of readers' sympathies. The Victorian poet, Matthew Arnold, as Lewis noted in *The Personal Heresy* (1939) and in *Unreal Estates* (1962), prophesied that literature would take the place of religion and become, as Lewis suggests, subject to "monstrous exegesis".

Now, some would say, we have moved on from there so that moral stridency and 'religious' energy are found in politics and the 'cancel culture'. One writer[3] has suggested that those considered to have committed 'secular blasphemy' are not only excommunicated but are subject to 'virtual vigilante action' which not only silences the apostate but creates a culture of fear of speaking out.

It is only a small step from recommending that Christians take literature a little less seriously than some do, to expressing a view about the commonplace categorisation of books into "High brow" and "Low brow" – books thought to be intellectually and somehow morally superior and those seen as mere entertainment for the less literate. The topic exercised Lewis throughout his career

---

3 The novelist, Chimamanda Ngozi Adichie in a Reith lecture. See *The Times* 8/12/22, p.32

and remains an issue today.[4] Literary snobbishness is far from dead. Is a difficult and highly literary book somehow 'better' than a thriller? And is it 'better' to read one than the other?

Lewis's own taste in reading was eclectic and his erudition never prevented him enjoying popular fiction and "thrillers" as well as books often read to, or by, children. He thought many examples written in these genres were very good, even great, books. What had become known as 'lowbrow' writing was by no means, in his opinion, necessarily bad writing. To assume that it was, he suggested, was a confusion of degrees of merit with differences of kind. The confusion is made worse by schools and universities which tell students what to think about "the great works" that they dutifully read. Having failed to recognise either the jokes, the tragedy, the romance or the lyricism, the student attributes the book's reputation to a mysterious element called "Style". They imagine this to be a sort of pedantry or abstruse literary magic rather beyond their comprehension but which admits the book to the canon of great works. Such a thing, says Lewis, does not exist as they imagine it. Imperfections of style, he explains, are not failings in some superadded grace but are the result of insensitive or careless choice of words. A poor choice in epithets, an ill-chosen metaphor, a sea of superfluous words, a lack of fluidity or rhythm, mean that the picture the author wanted to convey does not imprint itself on our imagination as it might have. Where a book interests us sufficiently to keep us reading but partly fails in these sorts of ways, that book is "defective in style".

---

4 The essay *High and Low Brows* was first published in *Rehabilitations* and is a prelude to the much later *An Experiment in Criticism*.

HIS LITERARY CRITICISM, HISTORY, THEORY

This is such crystal-clear advice about writing that one wishes it were the central tenet of all writing courses at university and school. Unless we, as writers, are enabling our readers to see what we see, feel what we feel, then our style is in some sense 'defective'.[5] There is no formula for good writing save one that enables the above.

The essay then moves on to consider the writer's motivation and the effect of time on our perceptions of literary value. Of the work that has survived the ages, Lewis notes that the vast majority was written either to edify or to entertain – by giving their readers what they wanted. The inescapable and ironic conclusion is that the 'lowbrow' writers of an earlier age most often become the highbrow writers of a subsequent one. Shakespeare is the most obvious case in point but citing contemporaries, Lewis wonders whether his own age may be remembered as that of popular novelists John Buchan and P. G. Wodehouse rather than that of the 'difficult' modernist poets, T. S. Eliot and W. H. Auden – thereby pointing up the ephemeral nature of intellectual fashions, something he loved to do. In fact, Lewis concludes, disparagingly, "difficulty" seems to be the factor which, in his day, admitted books into the 'highbrow' class. In the case of Virgil or Malory it is the patina of time which supplies it. For the modernists, if a commentator is needed for us to understand them, a passport into the pantheon is likely to be their reward.

Lewis foresaw a world in which both the writing of imaginative literature and the criticism of it become not so much a delight as

---

5 In a 1963 interview Lewis told Sherwood E. Wirt that the two essentials of 'style' were to know exactly what you wanted to say and then to make sure you said that exactly. See *God in the Dock* (Eerdmans, 1970) p.219. Fox in *Till We Have Faces* says similarly that this is the whole "art and joy" of writing. See p.305

an "accomplishment"; a world in which experts ensure that what is popular is also seen as being poor or bad writing. The idea of a spontaneity of delight in literature will not occur to such people because they have no experience of it. Good taste will only have been acquired by hard work and therefore will be held on to with "uneasy intensity". Those who approach literature simply from a love of it will be seen as dilettantes. Curiously, this has theological parallels that Lewis, of course, deplores. If what is popular is always bad then our taste as readers is, by nature, wrong and needs converting. The good critic is one who is washed, by long training, from the Original Sin of their Original Taste. Here again, we can see the recurrence of the idea of literature (or more widely, culture) taking the place of religion as Matthew Arnold had foreseen.

Fortunately, there is a cure that can be exercised by professional critics and private readers alike. Exercising a little patience, a little humility, and avoiding vanity and the laziness which leads us to over-simplify is the way forward.[6] We must recognise, Lewis states, both the good and the bad in any lowbrow book just as we should in any highbrow book. The very same kinds of goodness and badness are to be found in both categories. To think an 'easy' book (the sort we might read when ill) is bad just because it is 'easy' is a fundamental error.

At the end of the essay Lewis appends a long footnote in which he makes clear that the age of the perceived need for literary 'conversion' was already upon them and that the misleading distinction between highbrow and lowbrow had helped produce

---

6 It is interesting that Lewis summons the need for individual morality to his aid here. He adopts the same position as a reader that he had adopted for Scott and others as writers. Namely, a refusal to allow self-importance to become a dominating interest in both the reading and writing of books.

it. He adds that, in his experience, members of the *intelligentsia* were unable to speak of their 'inferiors' without contempt. Where there is a quarrel, he reminds his readers, reconciliation is the responsibility of the more reasonable of the disputants, *jure divina* – by divine law.

This is an extraordinarily prescient and important essay. Lewis was scathing about what University courses were doing to 'bewildered' and unwitting English Literature students over eighty years ago and would not approve of what has continued to happen (in terms of the usage of critical apparatus) since his death. Many courses exist today which omit most of the great works and many students read far more criticism than they do the works which it describes. A spontaneous response to the raw text is very often not the focus of study. The result is that a student may be acquainted with endless extracts from an anthology of criticism about, say, Shakespeare's tragedies but only have read *one* of those tragedies, a single time, and be quite unacquainted with the others. Yet 'tragedy' such a student might count as their 'speciality' or 'special subject'. How this can be considered an improvement on reading what Shakespeare wrote is unclear to me.

POEM NOT POET

One of the contentions Lewis strove to defend throughout his life was that it is not necessary to know about the poet in order to understand the poem (or other work). This is a controversy that is highly topical at present with sharply different views being taken in a society where 'cancel culture' – the practice of blacklisting or 'cancelling' certain writers because of the views they held (or hold) or the lives they have led – has hit the headlines. Once again, Lewis was ahead of his time in being ready to defend the poet, not on the grounds of morality but in a different way.

C.S. LEWIS ON LITERATURE

The Personal Heresy: A Controversy (1939) was Lewis's third academic book (with E. M. W. Tillyard). It defended a characteristic viewpoint which Lewis maintained throughout his career. Namely, that it is not safe to say that a work is an expression or reflection of the author's personality – an idea that at first sight will seem counter-intuitive to many today. Some of the chapters were published as early as 1934-5.

Lewis recounts that during the First World War he encountered an anthology of the soldier poets which promised to reveal things about them never before told. The assumption being that in reading their poetry we would find ourselves, as it were, in intimate conversation with them. This, Lewis perceives, is part of a trend in literary biographies to connect life and work in a way that the famous literary 'Lives' written by Dr Johnson never did. Today, in Lewis's time and our own, the widespread belief is that poetry expresses the personality of the poet. By contrast, Lewis took the view, not only that in poetry we have no representation of the poet, but often no representation even of any personality. It's an unusual view.

A seventeenth-century poem by Robert Herrick (*Upon Julia's Clothes*) serves to make Lewis's initial point which is that since the first object presented to us in the poem is silk, and that only secondly do we think 'What sort of man would have described silk in that way?' it must be the case that the poem has already affected our imagination and our idea of the poet cannot be part of that original effect. The only genuinely *poetical* experience is an apprehension of Julia's clothes. Subsequently we have a perception of the poet's skill and then, doubly removed from the poetry itself, thoughts about the personality of the poet which we infer from that skill. Lewis then produces a similarly philosophical, though

HIS LITERARY CRITICISM, HISTORY, THEORY

different, argument about a living writer's work, Walter de la Mare's poem *All That's Past*. He argues that since the poem is about the extended ages of humanity's history, the object of the poem cannot possibly be the poet who is one of the least important details in the concept.

This may seem highly academic but it reveals Lewis's philosophical way of thinking and is also important in freeing up our appreciation of much writing, which, if constrained too strongly by any negative view of an author's personality, will diminish the value of the poem, its genius, in reprobation. Our 'criticism' then will end up being partly of the life of the author, and not properly about the work as a separate entity at all. Twenty-first-century fascination with biography continues unabated and the sale of a book will often be boosted by a prurient or other interest in the writer's life.[7] The more sensational the life is, the more likely the work is to be read – irrespective of the quality of the writing.[8]

Lewis always liked to press home an argument that he felt was unassailable – whether in speaking or writing. True to form, in this instance he provides one further proof of his thesis, one which became fundamental to his thought – both critical and devotional – and appears in *Surprised by Joy* (Chapter XV), "Meditations in a Toolshed" and in many other places. The poet and the character presented in the poem cannot be one and the same because the presented character is one in the grip of an emotion while the poet has escaped sufficiently to represent it objectively, making poetry

---

7 Lewis wrote a poem about exactly this. See *Odora Canum Vis* in *Poems*, (Geoffrey Bles, 1964) p. 59

8 Things have come to such a pass in this that the footballer, David Beckham, on the eve of the publication of his 'autobiography' had no idea that his life story was about to be published! (Evidenced on BBC Radio 4, 9pm, 11/10/23, 9pm: When it Hits the Fan)

out of it. Someone crying out with pain, he tells us, is hardly the same as the one who expresses to the reader the nature of that cry. The poet writes about anger, sorrow or love, while the lovers or fighters or mourners live it. Lewis grants that we can grow close to the poet in such instances, that we can share "his consciousness" but only by looking *with* his eyes, not *at* them. We must look where the poet looks in order to do this; turning to look at him won't achieve it. We can "enjoy" him but not "contemplate" him. It is a distinction he found in Samuel Alexander's book, *Space, Time and Deity,* and reflection upon it played a significant part in his conversion.

We see here, not for the final time, that in order to enjoy our reading to the full and to read well, the underlying principle is that readers must subject their own personality and restrain a natural desire to impose oneself on a work, so that the world the writer wishes to create for us can work its magic. Even here, it seems to me, a theological truth is present: to be in awe of the created world around us is a better starting-point for understanding it than asking what one can get out of it. The precise analogies that Lewis finds by way of illustration are also always illuminating. One of several he gives here is that a window is not placed such that one might admire the window, but rather that we might forget the window in admiration of the landscape which it reveals. If we find ourselves looking at the glass, there is either something wrong with our eyes or with the glass itself.

Expressing their personality is not what poets do, even though they may do what no one else can. Personality is the point of departure, not the destination. The business of the poet is to reach and share with readers a "new mode of consciousness"; to negate limits of personality and psychology and take us to places of mind and spirit previously unexplored. In this way Lewis suggests that the writer is discovering at least as much as creating and the theory remains consistent with Lewis's view of originality. But of course, "personalities" hold pride of place in the imaginative literature of the world and Lewis is at pains to say that these are the last people he would want to exclude. All the people Shakespeare invented are to be treasured; it is Shakespeare himself Lewis would exclude from critical focus – though he accepts that there are blurred boundaries to the imaginative writing this rule applies to. Letters and some other classes of literature are borderline. Night and day remain useful distinctions even though at their frontiers they are indistinct.

The reason Shakespeare, or any other authorial personality, should be left out of the picture when considering fictional characters is simple: they are imaginary; he was real. When we read the plays we prepare ourselves for "feigning", for make-believe. The poet would be an intrusion into this imaginary world, a visitor from a higher plane, and to think of him at the same time as his creations produces an incompatibility of response: we must respond to the real quite differently from how we respond to the imaginary. We can "enjoy" the murder of a character on stage, even in some sense, the murder of a good character (as in a Shakespeare tragedy); but to do so in real life would be villainous. The distinction Lewis makes here is a useful one when starting to discuss our responses to, for example, twenty-first-century films which are ultra-realistic or violent, where our awareness of 'make-believe' or artistry is reduced to the minimum and the director's intention is to shock or appal. If we see such scenes, to what extent should we prepare ourselves to remember that the whole is part of an immensely painstaking construct where the actors involved may not even realise the nature of the final cut that audiences will be presented with?

Finally, Lewis adduces one further typically logical argument. If we are to take into account the writer's personality, then we either are in danger of confusing our delight in the work with our affection for the writer, or we have to try to disregard our antipathy and perhaps correct it.[9] Either way, the reader moves from the imaginative world to a world of ethics which depends upon data from history and moral principle. Making decisions about an author takes us forcibly out of the poetical, fictional world and away from the very thing we have opened the book to enjoy.

What Lewis calls "Poetolatry" he flags up as a danger as *The Personal Heresy* draws to a close. By this he means hagiographic studies of poets and the devotion which certain students have exhibited towards their latest hero. Today, we might say, the tendency is to debunk rather than worship, but as Lewis cleverly remarks, that's the other side of the same coin: "blasphemy is the child of religion". Matthew Arnold's prophecy had already come true as far as Lewis could see: poetry was acting as a substitute for religion.

What then, in the end, (Lewis asks in conclusion) is the *value* of literature? In terms of "the great mass" of people the answer is that it should be "interesting" in any one of a number of ways – as entertainment, or truth or fantasy. Lewis apologises that the answer cannot be more precise and then adds that it has been expected that it should affect us in a permanent way, not in any narrow moral way necessarily but in a profitable one, one which moves the reader towards other things they would like to "enjoy or do or be". This profit and pleasure criterion of course may tend to lower the

---

9 From different ages, Thomas Malory, Ben Jonson, Lord Byron, V S Naipaul and John Le Carré all spring to mind. The same could be said of some great composers and artists.

status of the poet but, paradoxically, this is precisely what may save poetry from extinction. Lewis is thinking here of the obscurity of the modernist fashion in poetry which precluded for him, and for many, the possibility of gaining either pleasure or profit from their work. We may have had to learn the lesson of *The Ugly Duckling* he admits, and see beauty where we had not expected to find it, but the time has come now to remember the lesson of another Hans Andersen story: one called *The Emperor's New Clothes*.

It is a powerful ending to a closely argued, little read, and important piece of Lewis's literary wisdom.

C·S·LEWIS

An Experiment in Criticism

CAMBRIDGE UNIVERSITY PRESS

CHAPTER TEN

STUDIES IN WORDS AND *AN EXPERIMENT IN CRITICISM*

If *The Personal Heresy* showed us Lewis dealing with large abstract concepts, albeit ones that directly affect the way we read, his much later *Studies in Words* (1960) is similarly about our reading but at the other end of the literary spectrum: the examination of how individual words have changed in their usage and meaning. Even here, however, Lewis's interest is far from merely lexical or even historical. He uses the ten words he selects to throw light on intellectual history, on the way ideas and sentiments have changed down the years. In some ways it is the most technical and most obviously erudite of his books and emerged from his lectures to students at Cambridge after his appointment there in 1954. Lewis deplored sloppy or careless reading (especially among fellow dons), and sought to educate his student audience into avoiding some of the worst pitfalls. Indeed, his stated aim in the book is that it is "an aid to more accurate reading".

For our purposes in this introduction I shall draw attention merely to some of his insights about the good and bad use of language generally, and about "the immensely potent instruments" that our language uses.

There is a simple rule which enables us to determine what is the best language. Since language is for communication, the language which allows for the clearest and greatest number of distinctions of meaning is the best. Thus the French word *aimer* is less useful than our words 'like' and 'love' both of which, in French, have to be inferred from the context. But language can also be diminished by popular usage, especially by "inflation". When a word ceases to be used or to have useful meaning in this way Lewis calls it "verbicide". He gives as examples the substitution of 'awfully' for 'very' and 'tremendous' for great. This is so commonplace now, three or more generations on from Lewis, that we hardly notice what has been lost. The American 'awesome' which can now be used in response to the most trivial pleasantry gives an up-to-date example of the process. Another means of verbicide is what Lewis calls "verbiage", when a word promises something that it never delivers. *Significant* is one such when it is used without the intention of telling the auditor what its significance is. *Diametrically* is another case when it is used simply as a superlative to *opposite*. If, sixty years on from Lewis's book, we have lost our awareness of these, would it be true to say that *literally* can still appal us when it is used in conversation as a preface to a metaphor or a gross exaggeration?[1] This process of verbicide, Lewis reveals, is caused by the fact that most are more concerned to express approval or disapproval than they are to describe. So words tend towards an evaluative use rather than a descriptive one. Ultimately the word becomes merely evaluative, simply another way of saying something is good or bad. The old word *villain* went through this process – as is shown in a later chapter.

Another process that Lewis explores is the way that context will insulate a word's meaning. Ghosts and fairies for instance are not in our minds when we see a shop notice advertising 'Wines and Spirits'. Nor, in a church, would we think of railways if we are contemplating the Stations of the Cross. Because of this, the semantic intruder, the unexpected and unintended use of a word which has a highly unsuitable and coarse usage as well as the

---

1 "His jaw *literally* hit the ground in his surprise." "His thinking was *literally* a million miles off."

intended one, has explosively funny results, Lewis admits, when used inadvertently by "a headmistress or a bishop". [2] It's a reminder that he had, on occasion, an earthy sense of humour. In addition, this insulating process allows old meanings to persist. We still talk of the *train* of a dress, as well as a railway train; or the *magazine* of a fortress as well as the word more commonly meaning a glossy periodical. Each survives because they live far apart.

One point, especially useful to those engaged in apologetics, is made about "tactical definitions". Lewis alerts us not only to the fact that a purely English dictionary may be subject to a lexicographer's viewpoint, but that when we read or hear definitions in literature other than dictionaries we should be even more wary. The very fact that the writer chooses to define a word should make us sceptical: we define words when we are departing from their normal current usage.[3] What other purpose would the definition serve – unless in a school book? In a book of instruction or a lesson we may be reminded that *deprecate* is not the same as *depreciate*, nor *immorality* mean the same as *lechery*, precisely because the two meanings are now being conflated. Further to Lewis's examples one might add the word *disinterested* which has never before meant *uninterested* but is now beginning to mean exactly that. Resisting the change is worthwhile if a useful word is about to be lost.

At the Fringe of Language is Lewis's title for his final chapter

---

2   In conversation with Kingsley Amis and Brian Aldiss Lewis tells the story of a bishop watching a performance of *A Midsummer Night's Dream* (in which the rustic character 'Bottom' appears) at a girls' school. In his speech he remarked unwittingly that it was the first time he had ever seen a female Bottom. (*C. S. Lewis on Stories and Other Essays on Literature* Ed. W. Hooper, Harcourt Brace Jovanovich, 1982) p.153

3   Lewis gives a perfect example of this in *Studies in Words* when talking about Alexander Pope's use of the word 'wit'. (pp.106-7)

in *Studies in Words*. He touches on a number of issues at the start including the limitations of language in describing complex physical shapes; its limits in a complex but sudden shift in circumstances (in which an adequate description of the complexity destroys the suddenness of the change[4]) and the use of emotional language. This last topic he shows to be often misunderstood in so far as many sorts of statement are judged 'emotional' when in fact they are not so. Often they are statements of fact which arouse an emotion or value-judgements (such as "this is good") which are, rather, statements of approval or disapproval in which our *feelings* about what is judged good may not match the judgement. This is again a very useful reminder for Christian apologists today who can often be accused of using emotional language when they are not. Lewis even says that treating "I am washed in the blood of the Lamb" as being emotional language is wrong. Yes, it is a metaphor, but one that is being used to convey what the speaker considers to be a fact. An opponent would argue that it is a mistaken belief but it is so only in the way that a 'too previous' wartime rumour led to the error "Germany has surrendered". Those three words are not emotional but merely factual – the result of an emotion based on a mistake.

Moving on from this Lewis then gives good advice to any "beginner" in imaginative writing. He says we should all avoid the use of epithets that are "merely emotional". It is pointless simply to tell your readers that something was attractive or repulsive for instance; a quite different approach is needed: we must make our readers exclaim "how attractive" or "how repulsive" after we have evoked that response by the "right stimuli" – by our metaphors,

---

[4] On Ransom's arrival on Perelandra, Lewis, after six pages of description writes, "Words are slow" and lets us know that his hero had spent less than five minutes on Venus. (p. 40 Ch.3)

by the very rhythm and melody of our prose and by the length of our sentences – whether brief or long. *Telling* needs to be replaced with *showing*. When it comes to dialogue or speech, as opposed to description, whether in poetry, prose or drama, the purest writing is actually *mimesis* – imitation of human speech at its greatest moments of crisis.

Lewis then considers the matter of swear-words and abusive language which prefaces his remarks about writing criticism. A whole class of swear-words are words passing out of the domain of language proper into inarticulacy. Words with "the whole Christian eschatology" in their background, such as the complaint 'damn' or the abusive 'damn you' are not now used to consign our enemies to eternal fire and are emptied of almost all meaning thus nearly ceasing to function as words at all. Other terms of abuse have followed similar paths. The term *villain* was first used to describe your enemy as a *villein* – a person of low rank. *Cad* and *knave* assigned your victim to the servant class because they once meant boy or junior, that is, your inferior. Though not now used, a servant in the 'waiting' role in France was always referred to as *garcon*. In this way Lewis shows us that such language was used to show that our enemies were people to be looked down on. The words hurt because hurting was only part of what they did. They also evoked emotion because they stimulated imagination and the picture imagined was hurtful. Now of course they have become weaker because they do not accuse the object of anything in particular. They simply tell us the speaker is angry. To be called a *swine* no longer evokes the smell of the sty.

In this way a linguistic principle is established: in most cases, emotional words need to do something more than being merely emotional. In language therefore, hatred is its own worst enemy:

as everything gets pushed out of the word except the emotion it finally ceases to be useful. In the twenty-first century, we might add, where swearing is so commonplace, such words are the worst sort of clichés. For many speakers the words act simply as fillers because they have no other word available to them in their very limited vocabulary.

It is noticeable that there is absolutely no prudery in Lewis here. From the moral point of view he sees it as far more dangerous to use language emotionally when pretending to be merely conceptual than it is to be inarticulate by using swear-words. Terms such as *fascist* or *capitalist* or *bourgeois*, he tells us, are often used to insult rather than describe. They pretend to have intellectual content when they are merely being used to vilify. We must avoid doing the same when we find ourselves writing criticism.

When we find ourselves hating a work we need, as in so many previous situations mentioned, not to put ourselves forward, not to indulge our hatred, but rather to get oneself *out* of the picture: to show up the reasons for our dislike; to exhibit the faults of the writing rather than vilify them or the author. The critic's problem is that it is easier to do the latter and seems more immediately satisfying. Our desire to hurt can overcome our desire to be fair and our aim can degenerate into annoying the author rather than informing the reader. Thus, if a work is claiming to be a mature view of something, the temptation is to call it *adolescent* – not because it shows those traits but because that's exactly what the author hoped no one would say or think. *Adolescent*, Lewis explains, is not a good critical term anyway for it suggests a cause for why the book is bad rather than pinpointing the badness itself. *Provincial* is another example. The fact that the author lived or wrote as from one of the provinces (i.e. outside London) is not of itself a fault;

we need to know how this exhibits itself negatively in the writing. Better pejorative words are *monotonous* or *dull* or *hackneyed* which describe a particular fault directly. Wrong usage of this class of critical terms – using them to hurt, not describe – moves them into being "*mere* pejoratives", simply synonymous for *bad* and subject to the same process as *villein* described above.

This analysis by Lewis may well remind us of a principle that he believed ran through the whole of human experience. Whether in academic writing or in the hurly-burly of life, when hatred is indulged it over-reaches itself and, in the end, becomes impotent. Something like this can be seen at work in Lewis's fictional evil characters as their personalities fall apart or implode. He sees the principle at work supremely in Milton's depiction of Satan in *Paradise Lost* – as we have already discovered.

We must therefore, Lewis concludes, avoid such self-indulgence. When we admire an author but are disappointed by a particular work we should proceed with caution. But when the book comes from a writer we positively dislike it is better to keep silence for there is too great a likelihood that the book has touched a raw nerve and part of the fault may be in ourselves. Ever practical, Lewis suggests, if necessary, writing the review and then binning it a couple of days later when our blood has cooled.[5]

The Experiment

An Experiment in Criticism (1961) is in many ways one of Lewis's most counter-cultural academic books. It is a powerful

---

5 Lewis's own practice was to be generous to those critics with whom he disagreed. A good example is his high praise of Denis Saurat whose views he deeply opposed but to whom he paid genuinely high compliments. See *A Preface to Paradise Lost* p.91, Ch. XII. He is equally courteous to E. M. W. Tillyard. See *The Personal Heresy* p.49, Ch. III.

riposte to the dominant school of thought of the time (especially in Cambridge) which produced a canon of authors that had to be admired and which held very prescriptive views about 'good' and 'bad' literature. Lewis contends, in a sort of reversal, that books should be judged instead by the kind of reading they elicit rather than by a group of elitist critics who evaluate them.

After two short preliminary chapters concerned with frequently mistaken ideas about books and readers, Lewis gives us his own responses to pictures in books he loved as a child – the illustrations to Beatrix Potter's stories or Arthur Rackham's very different pictures for *The Ring*. Both these acted as substitutes or representations of a reality he would have preferred. He attended little to the pictures, using them, unthinkingly, as a launch-pad for his imagination and emotions. Most people always see pictures like that. We tend to enjoy representations of things that would please us in the 'real' world. Admittedly, we may also admire the artist's skill but such comments soon cease and the painting becomes like the novel we read once and then have little use for: it fills a space on the wall or a gap on the shelf.

This is 'using' art rather than laying ourselves open to it, says Lewis. To appreciate something properly we must not make it the vehicle for our own preoccupations and associations. We must instead look to see exactly what is there. We must surrender ourselves.[6] An unliterary reader, like most people with paintings,

---

6 This process of surrender, part of the self-forgetfulness that has been such a dominant theme throughout this selection, has its counterpart in the theological writing and fiction as well, nowhere more so than at the conclusion of *The Problem of Pain* where Lewis speaks of "continual self-abandonment" and surrender of oneself as being the law of heaven (p.139). He also describes this as an "unveiling" – which happens to Orual at the conclusion of *Till We Have Faces* – both literally (p.289) and then metaphorically (p.305). The image of the veil is also repeatedly used in *The Pilgrim's Regress*.

will never really discover whether or how a book is good or bad because such readers are always trying to extract what Lewis calls "the Event". All the subtle invitations which the chosen words give us in terms of imagination and feelings and concepts they have no use for. The unliterary look for the instantly recognisable and prefer the cliché because of this. In a brilliant example Lewis suggests that a hackneyed expression such as "my blood ran cold" is little more than a hieroglyph – a pictogram for fear. Any attempt to do more than this, to make 'concrete' any particular fear, falls on deaf ears for it offers readers what they do not want.

All this, it would seem, places a high value on the reader, and in particular on reading correctly, in such a way as to enable the writing to change us. In this respect Lewis's theoretical position has similarities to that of Richards and Leavis but with the difference that the criterion for judging what is good literature is writing that is capable of being read well; that to which we can respond fully in the terms the author would want and which is satisfying by the enlargement of our personalities, our being, rather than being mere castle-building for the ego or the fulfilment of our own personal and perhaps passing needs.

Myth

In the next chapter he deals with Myth. This genre of writing had from the earliest days captivated Lewis and became important to him as a way of apprehending reality. By comparing the summary narratives of the Orpheus story, Homer's *Odyssey*, and of several novels, he shows that there is a particular sort of story which has a value in itself – one which is independent of its incarnation in any literature. He defines how he will be using the term in a list of identifiers that is a useful point of reference whichever of his works we may be reading. A myth, he says, is (at least for the purposes of his current book) "extra-literary", hardly depends on suspense or surprise but rather has a sense of inevitability, often with a minimum of narrative. In myth, there is minimal identification with the characters. Though we feel a deep relevance between the events in our story and theirs, there is little sympathetic feeling. Orpheus's story makes us sad for all men, but not especially so for him. In addition, myth deals with preternatural matters, is always "grave" and never comic, is numinous and inspires awe.

Lewis is not concerned with the pre-history of myths or how they arose, only with how they act on imaginations and minds like our own; with myth which is the object of contemplation but not of belief or part of religious ritual. Nor is he trying to set criteria by which stories can be classified but rather to distinguish the different ways we read. To one, a story can be just an exciting "yarn" which is read in order to find out what happens; to another, the same story can convey a myth which never loses its power over us. Lewis cites Rider Haggard's work as a case in point. One reader will receive those stories like one of John Buchan's thrillers, another will pause and reach through to the myth beyond. By way of illustrating the idea that myth is "extra-literary" Lewis comments that Buchan is a far better writer than Haggard, but not a writer of myth – for that involves the creation of images which strike deep below the surface of our minds.

Christian readers will be reminded of Lewis's conception of "true myth"[7] and "the Myth that became Fact" in the pages of the New Testament. There, he believed, we find a story of extraordinary

---

7 The expression is used as early as 1931 in writing to Arthur Greeves where Lewis tells his friend that the Christian story is a myth with a huge difference: "it really happened". See *They Stand Together*, ed. W. Hooper (Collins, 1979) p.427

power and relevance and one that depends hardly at all on the manner of its telling. The very concept of God's incarnation in the place he created for us, and his death at our hands, is a true myth that can make the profoundest of impacts on the mind and heart. Yet some remain unmoved. For them, the approach to the 'evangel' must be a different way.

Escapism

Lewis was concerned that readers should not be misled by accusations of "escapism" when reading. All reading, he reminds us, is an escape from our immediate surroundings into a world of ideas or imagination. What matters is what we escape *to*. Both literary and unliterary readers will escape and doing so by no means suggests that they will be inactive in the real world. Some of the most "impossible" and distant worlds were created in the sixteenth and nineteenth centuries by men most active in everyday affairs.

Often enough, unrealistic work is also judged to be childish and this is a criticism Lewis had good cause to explore. He makes two points. The first is that, as his friend Professor Tolkien had already established, most fairy-tales and the great fantasy stories were not aimed at children at all, but at everyone.[8] Fashions in reading come and go, but children know what they like and are not put off by any atrophy in their elders' taste for such stories, which, just as with adults, some like and some do not. 'Age-related' literature may be useful as a guide in schools and libraries but it is a very fallible one. Today we might say that Lewis's own contribution to the genre, *The Chronicles of Narnia*, remain a perfect example of the principle. Reading the stories first as children, countless adults return to them again and again.

---

8 'On Fairy-Stories', *Essays Presented to Charles Williams* (Oxford University Press,1947), p.58

With characteristic precision Lewis makes his second point – surely one that we find expressed with such clarity only from him. If *childish* is to be used as a term of disapproval we need to ensure we mean by it only those things we are glad to outgrow – perhaps ignorance or jealousy. For we also know that childhood is marked by a curiosity that is tireless, a soon-to-be-lost intensity in imaginative power and a facility for wonder, for pity, and for admiration. Losing our 'childish' appetite for the adventurous and marvellous is hardly a matter for congratulation any more than losing our hair or our hopes.

To think of fantasy therefore merely as childishness is not to think sufficiently at all. In criticism, as in his apologetics, Lewis exposes some commonplace viewpoints as meaning very little and hardly worthy of consideration once the lack of logic behind them has been exposed.

In Chapter IX of the book, Lewis sums up the position he adopts under the title *Survey*. His five main points are as follows: "using" art rather than "receiving" it may brighten or palliate our lives but makes no addition to it; in the case of reading there is always an imagining of something non-verbal, the *content* of the words. "Users" find this a means to a further end – perhaps as a pastime or a philosophy of life – while "receivers" want to enjoy and rest in that imagined world: it is an end in itself in the way that, on a higher plane, a religious contemplative experiences the immaterial. Because of this "users" find words to be mere signposts towards the experience they want while the good reader of a good book finds words to be so exquisitely compelling and evocative that the metaphor of "magic" is entirely apt. This good reading is aural too: the sound of the words, in verse or prose, is part of the meaning. Lastly, "egoistic castle-building" will not be a long-lived

HIS LITERARY CRITICISM, HISTORY, THEORY

experience for someone who is reading well.

In keeping with everything else we have seen from Lewis on literature, before he ends this section he reminds us that in fiction, whatever else is provided, there must always be "entertainment". If a book can't provide that – whether playful or gripping – then there is no reason to look for any "higher qualities". It would be hard to miss here an oblique swipe at certain modernist writers who Lewis believed were simply bad, and the critics' enthusiastic reception of them as another example of *The Emperor's New Clothes*.

On Criticism[9]

Before the end of the chapter Lewis issues one caveat about literary criticism as an exercise in schools. The danger of it, he feels, is that it is an impediment to reception and forces boys and girls to keep on expressing an opinion. It is hard to avoid the logic of his view that we have to let a work take effect upon us before we evaluate it, otherwise there is nothing to evaluate. As always we have to keep ourselves out of the lens otherwise we can't see what we are looking at. Regarding each work "with suspicion" is especially fatal; we have to risk being deceived about an author's worth or intention if we are to be "receivers". The habit of continual distrust is as destructive in literature as it is in life. The best antidote in both cases is to put ourselves in the way of honest people and good books.

What is the good of reading?

As we reach the magnificent conclusion to *An Experiment in*

---

9 For a longer discussion of the topic, see Lewis's unfinished essay *On Criticism* in *C. S. Lewis on Stories and Other Essays on Literature*, ed. W. Hooper (Harcourt Brace Jovanovich, 1982) pp. 127 – 141

Criticism, his last book of critical theory, we are given a glimpse of something that explains in part why Lewis was such a great man as well as critic. It is a fitting note on which to end this introduction.

In rejecting the view that literature is of value primarily for what it tells us about life or in making us more cultured, Lewis realises that readers may think it is merely about pleasure or a separate aesthetic experience quite distinct from the practical world. He therefore lays his "few and plebeian" cards on the table while reminding us that there is no obligation to do so. For what mathematician is required to justify the value of his discipline? What cook to justify the value of good cooking? That sort of question belongs to a more over-arching enquiry. Nevertheless, Lewis will enter the fray.

He begins by comparing the broad question of what the good is of reading what people write to the question of asking what the good is of listening to what is said in a conversation. Unless we already have in ourselves all the advice, entertainment, information and fun that we want, the answer is only too obvious. If we take the term 'literature' less broadly then we must remember that it is both something *said* (*Logos*) and something *made* (*Poiema*). As the former it will tell a story or reveal or evoke an emotion. As the latter, by its beauty, unity, balance or contrasts of its different parts it becomes an *objet d'art*, designed to satisfy. Poiema cannot exist without Logos and must build its harmonies and imaginative unity around it. The pity and terror we experience in *King Lear* we can only feel as we know his story and imagine him in the storm – shaped by the words presenting the storm, his rage, his whole circumstance.

HIS LITERARY CRITICISM, HISTORY, THEORY

The distinction between Logos and Poiema is a useful one not least for those who want to retain a degree of objective standards when subjecting themselves to literature. It reminds us that Art is not Nature and that writing evokes a response or calls us to reflect upon something non-verbal: the world which we apprehend. The literature we read is not itself the truth but something which conveys the truth to us. As such, if in the reader's judgement it does not do this in any respect, though the work may be beautifully made, its value will be limited. The poet is not someone with a superior moral consciousness but a creature like ourselves but with a distinct gift as "makere". Reading or writing literature is not a means to superiority in any moral sense at all.

Nevertheless, what marks out "strictly literary" reading, Lewis tells us, is that we do not *have* to approve or even believe the Logos presented. We do not believe Dante to have depicted the real universe; we cannot believe that Housman and Chesterton are *both* right in their view of life but we may read them both. What good then, Lewis asks, is there in filling our time and minds with stories of what did not happen, and things which cannot exist? What good is there in the Ancient Mariner's fantasy of the skeleton ship?

The answer, or the nearest Lewis says he has got to one, is that each of us (who read) is searching for "an enlargement of our being".[10] Put simply, one of the functions of any art is to present us with that which the necessary narrowness of our actual lives must preclude.[11]

---

10 The corollary of this, presumably, is that for those who do not read (or use alternative means of being reached by the world's artists), either by choice or by innate intellectual or other limitation, this 'enlargement' cannot take place. But even this does not imply any moral or spiritual superiority, merely difference – and that is self-evident and useful.

11 See Lewis's *C.S. Lewis on Stories and Other Essays on Literature*, ed. W. Hooper (Harcourt Brace Jovanovich, 1982) p.10

C.S. LEWIS ON LITERATURE

As monads we see the world through the illusion of perspective and can see everything only from the peculiar viewpoint of our own minds. But somehow we crave windows, even doors, on to other worlds. Literature in the form of Logos provides those. We may feel we have "got out" or "got in" but either way we have escaped our solitariness and made the discovery: the world looks different from this vantage point. When we read well there is intellectual activity because we understand better the facts as they are rather than as we see them. There is also moral activity because we place ourselves in another's shoes which is what is involved in every just or charitable action. Finally there is love because that involves escaping from one self into another.

Our primary instinct is to promote ourselves but a secondary impulse is to leave the self behind, to counter its provincial and partial view, to find healing for the lonely soul. This secondary nature we can nurture in receiving art, in love and virtue and in knowledge. We might describe the process of self-forgetfulness in order to find enlargement as a paradox, but it is one that we have always known: 'he that loseth his life shall save it.' In this way, to enter the world of another's mind, to occupy in the theatre, for a moment, someone else's seat and use their glasses to scan the stage is a delight. Not all the views from that seat are worth having; others will be awe-inspiring and beautiful or terrifying and full of pathos, but it is literature that has provided them. Not always do we realise just what a debt we owe to the books we have read.

In the final paragraph of this late, great book, Lewis provides, in my judgement, an epiphany for the responsive reader. He speaks of how reading can heal the wound of our individuality without destroying its privilege, in a way that the mass emotion of a crowd can never do. Taking the image of the stars in a night sky from a Greek poet he suggests we see with countless eyes, become a thousand people, yet miraculously remain ourselves.[12] Here is transcendence – as in worship or love, in knowledge or moral action – but in transcending myself I also become and find the self I had always been looking for.

---

12 There is a strong verbal echo of this in the final pages of *Till We Have Faces* where Orual realises that Psyche, in having given herself over to death is still "the old Psyche" but now "a thousand times more" herself than she was. (p.317)

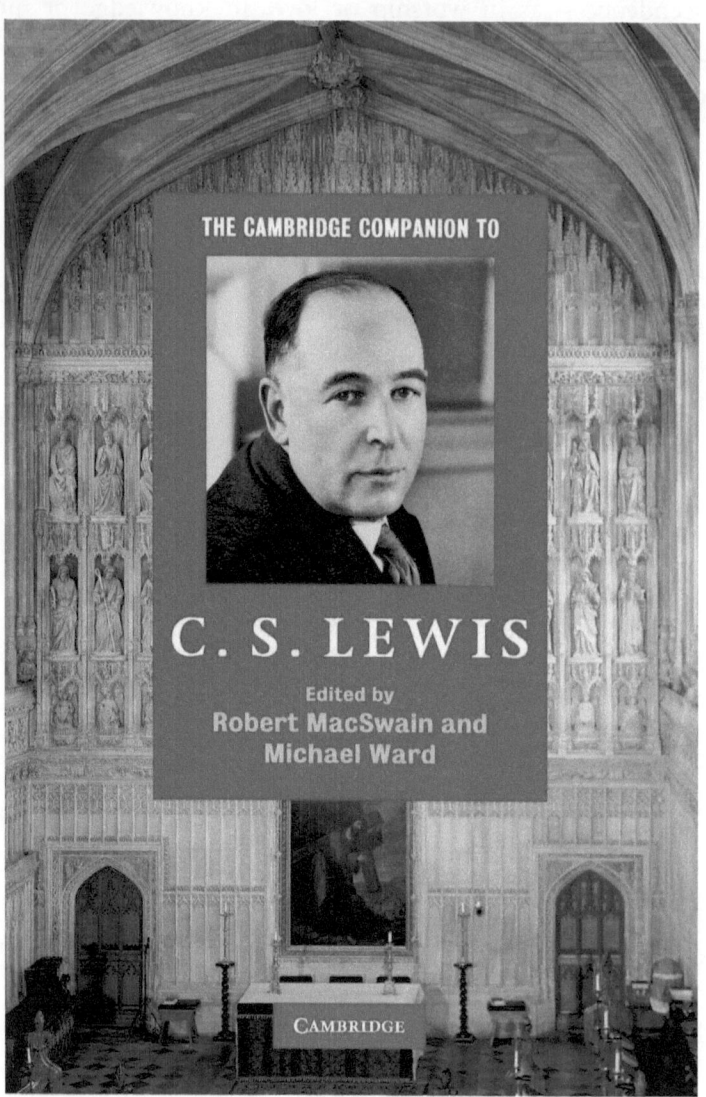

POSTSCRIPT

The summaries and reflections found in this book constitute only a tiny fraction of Lewis's published academic writing. In all this amounts to some 2,800 pages – surely an astonishing output for any full-time teaching academic but especially so when Lewis was also writing apologetics, devotional books, fiction and poetry, as well as writing and answering thousands of letters by hand[1] during his thirty years at Oxford.

One hundred years on from the moment when C. S. Lewis conducted his first tutorial or gave his first lecture at the University what can be said, by way of summary, about his contribution through the academic essays, lectures and books we have considered in this introduction?

The first thing to note is that the work has crossed continents. Not just to America but wherever English is spoken in departments of English Literature across the globe from Australia to Japan and China, from Berlin to British Columbia. To ignore or be unaware of Lewis's impact on our understanding of key figures and periods in the history of our literature is simply to be out of touch with how literary criticism and history developed in the middle part of the last century. The medieval period as a whole, Chaucer, Spenser, the sixteenth century, Milton, are now understood differently because of his scholarship. *The Cambridge Companion to C. S. Lewis* on its own is sufficient testimony to this.

But *what* was it that his students, his readers, were finding in his work? And what is it that this anthology brings to today's

---

1 The three volumes of his *Collected Letters*, a monumental work edited by Walter Hooper, extend to over 3,300 pages.

readers? The answer is something which lies beyond mere academic study, mere expertise in reading. Lewis, unlike any other, shows us the *logos,* the meaning – of *what* we read; he shows too *how* we read, and what that means for our understanding of the fleeting time we have to spend here. His eye, as well as having an intense acuity for significant and revealing detail, was always searching for the landmarks and pathways in both familiar and unfamiliar landscapes. He understood the map of literature – its scale, contours, symbols. His familiarity with regions unknown or daunting to the rest of us enabled him to chart a course through imaginative, philosophical and historical writing of two and a half millennia.

Lewis remains a guide we can trust. He never pretends to know when he does not.[2] He is never self-important. He does not back off in the face of difficulty when he knows that a conclusion has to be drawn that many of his readers or critics will not like. He reassures his listeners by apt analogy that the concept he is presenting is one they already have at least an inkling of. He always points to the landscape or beauty of the work rather than his emotional response to it because he wants the reader to see it for themselves. And because we do see it, we want more, we want to enter the "other worlds" to which he introduces us. That is not just because of his perception and erudition but also the result of his skill in rhetoric as well as "style" – as we saw him define it earlier.

The themes to which he returns are many but a core number can be seen in the passages we have read. If I had to choose one which both undergirded and overarched his academic writing it would be this: that to read properly we have to deny or minimise instincts

---

2 See, for instance *A Preface to Paradise Lost,* p.88, Ch.XII, and *An Experiment in Criticism* p.111, Ch.XI

of the self. We see this, of course, in his explicitly apologetic and devotional writing but it runs throughout his purely academic work too. It is there most explicitly in the *Experiment* but finds expression in his earliest work where he states that imitation, not originality is the biblical expectation; it is there when he tells us the poet cannot be the subject of the poem. We see it too when he tells us neither art nor artist should be over-valued and that Christians will approach literature with a lighter touch than others. Self-important intellectual snobbery is utterly out of court: 'lowbrow' books can be good and 'highbrow' ones bad; any sort of 'poetolatry' or exclusiveness is the wrong approach and verges on making literature a substitute religion. When he expounds *Hamlet* to us he asks us to become again like children and enjoy the story and the atmosphere if we are to understand the play correctly. His delight in fairy-stories so enjoyed by children reminds us that their essence is profound and a deep source of pleasure for adults. What he says of the "grand palace" of *The Faerie Queene*, we might apply to all our reading: we must enter by the "low door".

There could hardly be a more biblical approach to literature, or to life, and as with everything about C. S. Lewis there is a unity about his writing and his personal life all too lacking in many other writers. The repeated injunction of the New Testament is that we must use this "low door" and enter the Kingdom by the narrow gate; the eye of the needle is the way forward. To enter our inheritance we must become like little children; if we are to inherit the earth we must become meek, for the mighty will be cast down from their seats. He who would be first must be last and we, like Christ, must become the servant of all.

C.S. LEWIS ON LITERATURE

C. S. Lewis, like no other, brought this great Christian truth into every aspect of his writing. It is, indeed, a treasure-trove – treasure in Heaven as well as on earth.

Essays Presented to Charles Williams

Edited by C. S. Lewis

Sayers · Tolkien · Lewis · Barfield · Mathew · Lewis

APPENDIX

C. S. LEWIS ON CHILDREN'S LITERATURE

For many, their first experience of reading Lewis came through one of the Narnia stories, in all probability, *The Lion, the Witch and the Wardrobe*. This triplet of nouns has passed into the language even for those who never got as far as reading the book. As we have seen, his belief in the value of preserving into adulthood some of the insights and attitudes of childhood runs as a rich vein through the ore of his critical writing. But Lewis also wrote four essays (for very different audiences) about his views on children's writing – about the way both they, and we, approach "children's literature". Given that we, eighty years on from the time of writing, have an enormous industry which creates books specifically for every age at school and that what was then considered acceptable for children to read on their own is now deemed (by some publishers and universities) necessary to preface with "trigger warnings" about kidnapping or murder for *adult* readers, his views usefully inform the current situation. They accord a very high place to stories and fairy-stories in particular.

The first of these essays, *On Stories,* appeared in *Essays Presented to Charles Williams* (published 1947) and could hardly have had more intellectual bedfellows. J.R.R. Tolkien, Dorothy Sayers, Owen Barfield and Gervase Mathew were among the contributors and Tolkien's essay *On Fairy-Stories* expressed the view that Fantasy was one of the higher, not lower forms of Art. Moreover, its depiction of things not in the primary world ("if that indeed is possible") was a virtue not a vice.[1] Lewis was therefore in good company when he chose, when speaking of "children's

---

1 Eerdmans edition, 1977, p.67

books", to claim that their ventures into the preposterous sent one back to the real world with renewed delight. One example that Lewis gives of children's percipience is that they want the same story read "over and over again". Not only is this comparable to the literary adult who will return to the best books many times, but it is an unconscious awareness that although, in a series of events, the *fact* of a surprise cannot be repeated, the quality of unexpectedness can be richly enjoyed as we see more of the means by which it has been created and how it has an impact on the rest of the story.

The term "story" is of course often associated with children's books and Lewis notes that when the story exists for the sake of the characters or for social criticism such literary forms have been much examined. But where "everything else" exists for the sake of the story, little attention has been paid. Yet where these stories work powerfully there can be a gradation into myth – with all the richness that that genre provides. "Momentary suspense" and the excitement for which such stories are often valued is ephemeral and quickly forgotten but the atmosphere of the whole world of giants, or pirates or "otherness" lasts a lifetime. It is this almost static quality rather than a sequence of events that is the central matter of the book. "Stories" therefore, far from being unimportant, play a significant role in literary experience – whether read by adults or children. Nor, in this genre, is it necessary to believe that the marvels really happen. Indeed, belief in their actuality could be a hindrance.

One further profound point from the essay should be included here. All thinking Christians, it is probably fair to say, struggle at some point with imagining a world where both destiny and free will are important theological (and scientific) concepts. But Lewis reminds us that a large number of stories have their denouement

HIS LITERARY CRITICISM, HISTORY, THEORY

in fulfilled prophecy – the most famous being that of Oedipus, in which the very action designed to *prevent* disaster is the means of bringing it about. In such stories we see how free will is the *modus operandi* (method of working) of destiny. "At some more central region" Lewis suggests, this could be what reality is like.

Many of the points I have raised here find their exemplification in Lewis's own stories. Repeatedly in this book footnotes and asides have drawn attention to the link between his academic writing and his fiction – whether initially written for children or for adults. In a powerful image at the end of this essay Lewis likens life to a story in which there is (as always) a tension between the theme and the plot. Both in real life and in stories, "something must happen" but in both we are also confronted by the fact that the adventure is taken over by everyday details. What we wanted was a state of being but the sequence of events can never quite give it to us in its entirety. In Lewis's image, the author's plot is likened to a net, meshed with time and events in order to catch the fleeting bird. It escapes us, but for a moment in the net we saw and marvelled at its plumage. This much the story can do, and it is perhaps more than many lives might achieve.

Five years later, Lewis wrote *On Three Ways of Writing for Children*. The essay deplores the commonplace idea that in writing for children, authors should give "the public what it wants" or what it is imagined that children *in general* want. Lewis Carroll and Kenneth Grahame and Tolkien, however, all wrote originally with a particular child in mind and their stories have a particular quality because they are born of a developing relationship with an individual. Lewis's own rationale in writing children's stories (the third way) was that he realised "the fantasy or…fairy tale" was the best genre for what he had to say. At what age you come to the story is irrelevant. Lewis agreed with Tolkien that 'subcreation' could be most fully exercised in a fantasy world and that this is one of humanity's "proper" functions. Lewis also believed that in creating non-human characters an author could bypass many novelistic conventions and present insightful human psychology within a briefer span than the novel thereby allowing children (and those who don't read at length) a grasp of character types and social history otherwise beyond their reach. He cites Mr Badger in *The Wind in the Willows* as an example. In addition, the fairy tale forces the author to put all the energy of the book into actions and words. Long authorial commentary and explication simply won't fit. Brevity (Lewis might have said) in this case really is the soul of 'wit' – in its old-fashioned sense of having one's wits about one: being intelligent.

Predictably, and to the delight of many, Lewis takes advantage of his title and moves on to defend such literature, and an adult's taste for it. He makes the very good point that to lose interest in fairy tales and find it in novels is not necessarily growth but merely change; but to add the one to the other certainly is growth. When it comes to the charge of such stories fostering a false view of the world, Lewis goes on the attack and claims that it is the "realistic" stories that deceive by their very *pos*sibility but their almost infinite im*prob*ability. "School stories" may be 'escapist', for their plots about success and popularity flatter the ego as readers picture themselves in the central role. By contrast, fairy tales are not. Their outcomes and events we do not expect in the real world, nor do we want dragons there. They belong in a different universe but can create a longing for it while making our own more enchanting. A real wood can, in imagination, become an enchanted one. This is a very different kind of longing from egotism: readers forget themselves as they enter the forest.

HIS LITERARY CRITICISM, HISTORY, THEORY

Lewis is particularly concerned about those who "do not wish children to be frightened". This he sees as the most "serious attack" on the genre. It is a view that has re-emerged vociferously in recent years with 'cancel culture' and trigger warnings placed on books that might be deemed as causing offence, discomfort or shock. As so often, Lewis sheds light on the issue by making a useful distinction. Those fearful of childish readers being frightened may mean one of two things: (1) pathological fears and phobias; (2) fears that we must protect the child from the knowledge that we live in a world of evil as well as good, a world of death and violence as well as adventure and heroism. It is the latter that Lewis believes is profoundly mistaken: escapism "in the bad sense". Since they are born into the world of the atomic bomb and terrible cruelties, let them, he argues, at least hear of the bravery of knights of old and blood shed in a noble cause; of "wicked kings and beheadings" and of villains destroyed at the end. Ordinarily, children want to be a *little* frightened and such little fears are a good part of growing up.

As for pathological and irrational fears, they are a quite different matter. We bring them with us from birth it seems (or from our earliest pre-literary experiences perhaps), and Lewis does not believe they can be controlled by literary means. Limiting a child's reading to stories without any alarming events in them would hardly banish such terrors. Lewis, in a rare piece of self-revelation, confesses that on balance, if the world of 'faerie' – of knights and giants and dragons – and the terrible night-fears that he suffered as a child could both be erased from his experience, erasing 'faerie' would be too high a price to pay for escaping the other. For in the fairy-tale alongside the terror there is also the sublime, the protector in shining armour – an altogether more uplifting literary experience than reading of the burglar being caught by the police.

C.S. LEWIS ON LITERATURE

Asking what today's children *need* by way of reading produces, to Lewis's mind, a wrong further question, namely, "What moral do I want to inculcate?" That is to assume a too superior attitude and a better question would be "What moral do I, the author, need?" For what concerns us, will concern our readers whatever their age. Nevertheless, better still is not to let the question arise for the pictures you have in your head will tell you what the moral is if there is one – without having to ask. Anything else is likely to be superficial, a dangerous approach, as we understand "on high authority" that children have at least as much wisdom as we have. The greatest of children's authors wrote their stories out of the "habitual furniture" of their imagination and thinking, from the elements of their experience which they shared with children irrespective of what they thought children should have placed in front of them by adults. In such areas we have an equality with children and in this regard, Lewis says, we should treat them as equals.[2]

In a short piece written for *The New York Times Book Review* in 1956 Lewis tells us more about how he first conceived the Narnia stories – an account that is now so widely known as not to need repetition here. First came the images ("a queen on a sledge" etc.) and only later the Form – a Form in which the events needed no love interest and eschewed psychology: the fairy tale with its severe restraints on length, its traditional nature, its refusal to include analysis and digression or high-flown vocabulary. Only at a third remove from the initial impulse came the idea that such a story might unfreeze conventional 'religious' feelings and strip them of their "stained-glass" aura. The only sense, however, in which the stories that became Narnia were specifically written for children

---

2 "I never wrote down to anyone" – *C.S. Lewis on Stories*, ed. W. Hooper (Harcourt Brace Javanovich, 1982) p.48

was that the author excluded material they would not appreciate. What was *included* was never intended to be below the attention of an adult.

At their best, stories of this kind have great power by presenting in concrete, palpable form experiences which were previously beyond us. In a word, they achieve Mythical quality. With characteristic modesty, Lewis does not claim to have achieved this, but merely to have attempted it. Readers of the Narnia stories might wish to disagree with Lewis for millions have found there a world that enlarges and enriches our own and an experience of the sublime which produces feelings of awe, humility and wonder they have found in no other writer.

The last piece, "On Juvenile Tastes", which Lewis wrote for the *Church Times* in 1958, is another combative short article which takes some of these ideas a little further. He re-states his case that children are not "a distinct *literary* species" who need an industry given over to their literary tastes. Historically, the taste which we now often consider childish, was once the delight of all readers. More specifically, the fairy tale *"proprement dit"* (properly speaking) was born at the court of Louis XIV of France, ending up in the nursery when it went out of fashion. Curiously, children still love the genre. One reason why adults do not enjoy them as they used to is because the literary canon – approved books – is "extremely jejune and narrow". Lewis is not often as bluntly condemning as this and the comment reveals the strength of his feeling by this date when the Cambridge *literati* were dominant in directing the educated public as to what might be allowed as best to read. But it is not just the insipid and vapid that Lewis condemns but also the lack of interest in narrative, the preoccupation with novelty, psychological ideas and social comment.

In conclusion Lewis, without reserve, divides children's writers into the "wrong sort" and the "right sort". The former see children as distinct from other readers and give them what they are supposed to like; the right sort see that children share a common ground with the rest of humanity – both past and present – and write about that.

When it comes to writing about children's literature we can therefore see that, as in almost every other area, Lewis likes to make oppositions or dualities, to divide the world he is presenting into two – whether he be talking about the Bible, or Milton, low and high brow tastes, or fairy tales. For some readers this is unnecessary or unsubtle. For others it is a way of seeing, even of spiritual insight, that comes with a Christian vision of the world. I suspect that Lewis himself would say that he saw things this way on the highest possible authority: for each of us, ultimately, has to tread one of only two paths.

POINTS AND QUESTIONS FOR FURTHER STUDY

CHAPTER ONE

1. Consider how Lewis manages to use a single text such as *Lord of the Rings* to open windows into other and larger worlds.

2. How does Lewis's definition or use of the word 'myth' differ from how it is commonly used today?

3. Using the term 'myth' as Lewis does, what books or stories can you think of which provide a deeper insight into a reality that mostly eludes us?

4. In what senses is it true that something or someone considered unimportant may hold the key or a clue to the meaning of things?

5. How far do you agree with Lewis that *Animal Farm* is a far greater book than *1984* in so far as it illuminates the whole human condition?

6. Kipling depicts Humanity as needing to be "licked into shape" before being useful. That, and his depiction of the cruelty and abuse in the normal work practices of a previous age would lead some publishers to provide 'trigger warnings' for readers. What is your view of that?

7. Is "the Inner Ring" something you have experienced? Does Lewis's analysis of it cast useful light on it?

C.S. LEWIS ON LITERATURE

Chapter Two

1. William Morris is not much read today. What does Lewis suggest here that might induce a reader get hold of one of his books?

2. Why do you think Lewis was as keen to defend the work of good 'Pagan' or non-Christian writers as those who shared his religious views?

3. Why has there been such a revival of interest in fantasy writing over the last thirty years or so?

4. "Longing" is a key theme in Lewis. What elements and causes of it do you find in this chapter or in the William Morris essay?

5. To what extent has the modern world obscured or negated the "haunting desire for immortality"?

6. What similarities and differences do you find between the search for meaning in the lives of Morris and Lewis?

7. Albert Camus wrote: "Beauty is unbearable, drives us to despair, offering us for a minute the glimpse of an eternity that we should like to stretch out over the whole of time." (Notebooks 1941-52). Is this an example of what Lewis found in common with Morris who experienced the "longing" that Lewis repeatedly wrote about?

8. We owe to Sir Walter Scott a way of thinking about the past. What does this have in common with Lewis's view of the past?

9. "Undeception" is a common factor in both the novels of Jane Austen and those of C.S. Lewis. To what, if any, extent, does this reduce the interest or value in the plots of either author? Is there a sense in which this enhances the novels?

HIS LITERARY CRITICISM, HISTORY, THEORY

Chapter Three

1. Why does Lewis call Joseph Addison, "historically momentous"? What evidence is there that we still, in certain respects, live in the age which Addison ushered in?

2. Why is it important, according to Lewis, for thinking Christians to recognise the "profound change in human sentiment" in the Romantic Movement?

3. What happens when we "overvalue" art?

4. *The Pilgrim's Progress* is one of the world's greatest allegorical stories. Why does Lewis consider allegory to be still very important?

5. What defence can be made for Bunyan's "narrowness" of view in his book?

6. In what respect is the "variousness of the translations" of the Bible a minor matter in relation to the subject matter, according to Lewis?

7. How does Lewis shed light on the erosion of society's basic knowledge of the Bible?

Chapter Four

1. Why is it a "serious misjudgement" to blame Milton for writing in such an "elevated" style?

2. What important ambiguity does Lewis wish to clear up about the "character" of Satan in the poem?

3. How does Lewis bring out the self-destructive nature of evil in Milton's poem?

4. "We either love or hate the poem according to how we react to the exposure it forces upon us". If you have read any parts of Paradise Lost would you say that was your reaction?

5. Would you accept David Barratt's suggestion (see footnote 10), that Lewis may inadvertently deflect our attention from the poem to himself by raising some of its theological difficulties?

HIS LITERARY CRITICISM, HISTORY, THEORY

Chapter Five

1. Why is "chronological snobbery" an important concept to be aware of?

2. How does Lewis reverse a popular conception today with regard to how we think of Puritans and Catholics in a previous age?

3. Why does Lewis think that's Donne's love poetry was (and today he would say still is) overrated by many critics?

4. What problem does what Lewis calls "variation" solve?

5. Would this understanding of "variation" help your appreciation when reading the plays or seeing them in performance?

6. What is "the first principle of all reading" and how is this applicable more widely?

7. Can you agree with Lewis that the subject of *Hamlet* is death? Does that exclude it from being about other things too?

Chapter Six

1. What profound change in moral concepts took place between the time of Aristotle (died 322 BC) and that of Seneca (died AD 65)?

2. By what route does that change lead to allegory?

3. How is it that allegory is "the only way certain stories can be told"?

4. How does Lewis's criticism here shed light on Jesus's "eye of the needle" image and parable?

5. "Plato frames *The Chronicles of Narnia*". Can you say how, and does this encourage you to read or re-read some of Plato?

6. What is there in Lewis's summary of the "value, beauty and significance" of Spenser's *Faerie Queene* that might mean that its appeal could return at some point to twenty-first century readers?

7. Are "The Kappa Element" and "otherness" important in your reading of Lewis? Where do you find these to be most powerful?

HIS LITERARY CRITICISM, HISTORY, THEORY

Chapter Seven

1. Why does the medieval period sit well with Lewis's approaches to criticism and originality?

2. How does Lewis demonstrate that the cosmology of the material universe as the medieval world conceived it was so satisfying to those who lived within it?

3. How is it that medieval cosmology does not support the mistaken view that the people of the time believed in the Earth's "high dignity"?

4. In what ways does this mistaken view inform the thinking of today's secular world?

5. Give an example of how "analogical language" today masks our similarity to the medieval world in certain respects.

6. Does *The Discarded Image* enhance your appreciation of Lewis's science-fiction trilogy?

7. Some would say they perceive the cosmos differently after reading *The Discarded Image*. Might it change your own view?

C.S. LEWIS ON LITERATURE

CHAPTER EIGHT

1. What "undeceptions" does *English Literature in the Sixteenth Century* seek to bring about in its opening section?

2. What insights does Lewis provide on the current debate about imperialism?

3. How did the voyages of discovery to the New World contribute to the erosion of the doctrine of Original Sin?

4. In what respects does a misunderstanding of Elizabethan Puritans impact on our society today?

5. Lewis spends time describing the spiritual experience of an early Protestant. Is this justifiable in a book of literary history?

6. In what sense did Tyndale see the purpose of the 'gospel' as being to save the world from morality?

7. What does Lewis contribute in this chapter to an understanding of "the greatest divide in the history of Christendom"?

8. "Every translation is an (often unrealised) implicit commentary." What two reasons are given for this statement? Does it suggest to you that the use of different versions of the Bible might be illuminating?

HIS LITERARY CRITICISM, HISTORY, THEORY

CHAPTER NINE

1. How do Lewis's views on "originality" differ from the widely held view of that concept today?

2. Which of these two views do you find more tenable, or more attractive?

3. Valuing literature for its own sake, Lewis suggests, is a "solemn vacuity". Are there sufficient grounds for agreeing?

4. "Literary snobbishness is far from dead". Can you cite examples to indicate the truth (or falsehood) of this?

5. How would you define "style" in writing, in the light of Lewis's views here?

6. Do you agree that it is the level of difficulty in reading a book which decides whether it is "highbrow" or not?

7. How do Lewis's views on the role of the personality of the poet in our reading of the poetry, "free up" our appreciation of any poem?

8. At the end of this chapter we see Lewis starting to answer a question about the value of literature that we shall come across again. What does he tell us here?

C.S. LEWIS ON LITERATURE

Chapter Ten

1. What have you found useful here, more than sixty years on from the point of writing, in Lewis's analysis of both written and spoken language in *Studies in Words*?

2. "Emotional words need to do something more than being merely emotional." Can you illustrate the truth of this from current commonplace usage?

3. In writing criticism, what are the initial principles to remember?

4. How does Lewis characterise "using" art rather than "receiving" it?

5. What, according to *An Experiment in Criticism* is the criterion for good literature?

6. How "myth" is used in the book Lewis defines quite exactly. Do you think this applies to modern writing as well as ancient?

7. How is the accusation of escapism dealt with in the book?

8. What dangers need to be avoided when teaching literary criticism in schools?

9. "What is the good of reading?" Has C. S. Lewis helped you answer this question?

C.S. LEWIS

Studies in Words

SECOND EDITION

CAMBRIDGE UNIVERSITY PRESS

INDEX

accurate reading, 133
Adam, 45, 46, 50, 51, 81, 105
Addison, Joseph, 34, 49
Aeneid, 47, 117
Age of Reason, 34
Alexander, Samuel, 128
allegory, 11, 37, 38, 73 - 85
Ambrose, 75
America, 28, 37, 42, 103, 104, 105, 107fn, 151,
Amis, Kingsley, 135
Andersen, Hans, 131
Animal Farm, 14
Anstey, F., 13
Aquinas, Thomas, 90
Aristotle, 73,74, 82, 90,91,92,93, 117, 119,
Arnold, Matthew, 25, 121, 124, 130
art as 'entertainment', 121, 130, 145, 146
art as religion, 121
art, 'using', 140, 144
Aslan, 29, 51
astrology, 102
Auden, W. H., 123
Austen, Jane, 28, 29, 30, 34, 49, 88

Authorised Version, 109, 112, 113
awakening, 28, 30

Barfield, Owen, 56fn, 66, 157
beginners, advice to, 136
Bennett, J. A. W., 3
Bible, 36, 37, 40-43, 56, 62, 109, 112, 113, 164
Blake, William, 35, 49
Book of Common Prayer, 113
Brewer, D, 2, 87
Brown, Dan, 72
Buchan, John, 123, 142
Bulverism, 118
Bunyan, John, 36-40, 113
Burke, Edmund, 35
Byron, Lord, 22

Calvin, John, 57, 106
Calvinism, 100
Cambridge, 1, 4fn, 25, 36, 133, 140, 163
Camus, Albert, 23 fn
'cancel culture', 121, 125, 161
Catholics, 34, 57

179

Chesterton, G. K., 39fn, 67fn, 147
'childish' as disapproval, 144
chivalry, 107
Christ, 41, 42, 61, 76, 78, 153
Christie, Agatha, 80
chronological snobbery, 56
Coghill, Prof. Nevill, 5, 45
Copernicus, 101
courses in English Literature, 63, 122, 124, 125
Courtesy, 83
Courtly Love, 87
Coverdale, Miles, 112
Cranmer, Thomas, 113
creativity, 25
Cromwell, Oliver, 46
Crucifixion, 76

Danielson, Prof. Dennis, 45
Dante, 82, 90, 147
Dark Tower, The, 18
Darwin, Charles, 97, 101, 107
death, 13, 63, 64, 66
De Descriptione Temporum, 4, 33, 87

definitions, special, 135
determinism, 95, 100, 102
Dickens, Charles, 108
Donne, John, 55-58, 63fn, 100
Doyle, Arthur Conan, 18
Duriez, Colin, 33

Elijah, 112
Eliot, T. S., 15, 24, 123
Elizabethans, 106
Empire, 104
Enlightenment, the, 34
Epic, 45, 46
Epictetus, 74
Erasmus, 112
Escapism, 12, 143, 161
Exodus, 74

fairy-tale, 12, 77, 78fn, 85, 143, 153, 157, 159 - 164
Fall, the, 74
fantasy, 12, 13, 75, 77, 78, 130, 143, 144, 147, 157, 159, 160
Fleming, Prof. J V, 3, 45, 99
Fowler, Alastair, 117fn
Freud, Sigmund, 101

Gabriel, 94
Gardner, Helen, 87
Geneva Bible, 41
Gibb, Jocelyn, 3, 45fn
Grace, 81, 95, 110
Great Divorce, The, 18, 40
Greeves, Arthur, 66, 142fn

Haggard, Rider, 18, 142
Hamlet, 58, 61-67
Hell, 40
Henry VIII, King, 113
Herrick, Robert, 126
Hobbes, Thomas, 105
Hooker, Richard, 100
Hooper, Walter, 5, 30, 76fn, 80fn, 85fn, 87, 95, 111fn, 135fn, 142fn, 148fn, 151fn
Homer, 47, 56fn, 82, 119, 141
Hough, Prof. Graham, 83fn
Housman, A E, 147
human rights, 16
humanism, 99, 100, 101, 106, 107

imagination, 3, 59, 76, 87, 104, 122, 126, 137, 140, 141, 143, 160, 162

Inner Ring, 15-18
intolerance, 39, 40
Israel, 74

joy, 13, 27, 55, 108, 122fn
Johnson, Dr Samuel, 126
Julius Caesar, 64
Justice, 82
Justification by faith, 106

'Kappa Element' 85, 127-128
'King James' Bible 36, 40-42, 109fn
Kingsley, Charles, 103
Kipling, Rudyard, 15-18
King Lear, 146
Kirkpatrick, W., 1, 79
language, good and bad, 133ff
language, limitations of, 136
Lawlor, J, 3
Leavis, F R, 52, 141
Letters of C. S. Lewis, 75fn
Letters to Malcolm, 118
literature as 'accomplishment', 123
Logos, 75, 146-148, 152
longing, 22, 23, 66fn, 93, 160

Lord of the Rings, 11
Luther, Martin, 57, 112

Macbeth, 59, 60, 65
Malory, Thomas, 123
Mantel, Hilary, 76
de la Mare, Walter, 126
Mary Tudor, 113
Materialists, 24
Mathew, Gervase, 157
Membership, 118
Milton, John, 6, 14, 36, 45-53, 82
mimesis, 119, 137
Miracles, 107
Montaigne, Michel de, 101
moral law, 110
More, Thomas, 41, 57, 111
Morris, William, 21, 65, 85
mortality, 22
myth, 11-14, 31, 75, 141, 163

Narnia, 2, 14, 19, 25, 29, 30, 77, 79, 143, 157, 162, 163
natural law, 58
Nature, 80, 97, 147
Nesbit, E., 13
New Testament, 64, 78, 109, 112, 113, 118, 119, 142, 153
'New World', 103

"Old Western", 36
originality, 88, 118, 119, 128, 153
Original Sin, 105
Orpheus, 141, 142
Orwell, George, 14
Othello, 64
other worlds, 6, 12, 56, 85, 152
overvaluing art, 25, 36
Oxford, 1, 2, 6, 107, 117

Parables of Jesus, 77
Pascal, Blaise, 94
Paradise Lost, 15, 84, 139
Pepys, Samuel, 16
Perelandra, 18, 31, 76fn, 80fn, 83, 91fn, 94fn, 95fn, 118fn, 136fn
personality, 14, 88, 89, 120, 125-9
Peterson, Jordan, 79fn
Piehler, Paul, 6
Pilgrim's Progress, The, 77
Pilgrim's Regress, The, 12, 37, 140fn
planets, 91, 94, 96, 102
Plato, 71, 79, 80, 90, 119

HIS LITERARY CRITICISM, HISTORY, THEORY

Poe, Harry Lee, 3fn, 87fn, 117fn
Poems of C. S. Lewis, 127fn
Poetolatry, 130
Poiema, 75, 146,147
polytheism, 73
Pontius Pilate, 76
Pope, Alexander, 105
Preface to Paradise Lost, A, 45-53, 71
Pre-Raphaelites, 21
Primum Mobile, 92
Problem of Pain, The, 25, 40, 140fn
Prophets, Old Testament, 74
Psalms, Book of, 59
Ptolemy, 92
Puritanism, new, 25fn
Puritans, 34, 46, 57, 100, 106, 107, 110

Ransom, Dr. Elwin, 31, 51, 52fn
Rational Piety, 34
reading, use of, 2, 4, 61, 78, 85, 126, 140, 141, 143, 144, 146-9, 161
Reality, 21
Reformation, 109
Renaissance, 55, 99
Resurrection, 76

Richard II, 62
Richards, I A, 52, 141
Romance, 12, 80, 88, 107
Romantic Movement, 35, 42
Romeo and Juliet, 64
Rousseau, Jean-Jacques, 105, 120

St. Augustine, 75, 105, 119, 120
St. John, 84
St. Paul, 66, 74, 84, 111
Saurat, Denis, 139fn
Satan, 45-51, 81, 139
Sayers, Dorothy, 14, 157
scepticism, 73
Schaeffer, Francis, 24
scholastic philosophy, 107
schools, literary criticism in, 145
Screwtape Letters, The, 31
Scripture, 38, 40, 43, 72, 106, 109
Scott, Sir Walter, 25-27, 124fn
self-expression, 119
self-forgetfulness, 140, 148, 160
Seneca, 74
Shakespeare, 34, 58, 75, 78, 84, 103, 123, 128
Sidney, Philip, 55

183

sin, 74

sincerity, 38

slave trade, 104

Socrates, 118

Socratic Society, 6

Spenser, Edmund, 55, 76, 77, 82, 83, 84

Statius, 73

Stoics, 104

story, 12, 29, 37, 47, 63, 73, 77, 131, 141, 142, 146, 153, 158, 159, 160, 162

'Style', 122

sublime, 35, 120, 161, 163

suffrage, 82

Surprised by Joy, 39, 81, 126

swear-words, 137

taste in reading, 122-4

telling and showing, 137

That Hideous Strength, 14, 18

The Last Battle, 77

Till We Have Faces, 23fn, 25, 27, 66, 76, 79fn, 110fn, 122fn, 140fn, 149fn

Tillyard, E. M. W., 125 139fn

Tolkien, Prof. J. R. R., 11,12, 76, 78, 157

translation, 40-42

Truth, 6, 22, 29, 52, 56, 72, 81, 84, 97, 120, 128, 130, 147,

Twelfth Night, 62

Tynan, Kenneth, 5

Tyndale, William, 40-42, 109, 110, 111, 112

undeception, 28, 30

unliterary reading, 140, 141, 14

value of literature, 130

value-judgements, 136

'verbicide', 134

Variation, 59

Victorian period, 18, 25, 36, 84, 101, 121

Virgil, 47, 48, 123

Ward, Michael, 45fn, 85fn

Watson, George, 6

Williams, Charles, 13, 56fn

Wodehouse, P G, 123

work, 15-17

Wilson, A. N., 1fn

Wirt, Sherwood E., 122fn

C. S. LEWIS

Selected Literary Essays

Cambridge University Press

LIST OF LEWIS'S NON-FICTION CITED

There are multiple collections of Lewis's essays, reviews and lectures in various forms. In the list below I give the original title and date of first publication of the volumes in which the writing cited in this book appeared. Providing the original date helps the reader to trace the development of Lewis's thinking. In the case of the four books of collected essays edited by Walter Hooper, the editor provides date and place of first publication.

The Allegory of Love (1936)
Rehabilitations And Other Essays (1939)
The Personal Heresy: A Controversy (1939)
A Preface to Paradise Lost (1942)
English Literature in the Sixteenth Century, Excluding Drama (1954)
Studies in Words (1960)
An Experiment in Criticism (1961)
They Asked for a Paper (1962)

Edited by Walter Hooper:
Studies in Medieval and Renaissance Literature (1966)
"The Genesis of a Medieval Book"
"Imagination and Thought in the Middle Ages"
"Edmund Spenser, 1552-99"

Selected Literary Essays (1969)
"Variation in Shakespeare and Others"
"Hamlet: The Prince or The Poem"
"Donne and Love Poetry in the Seventeenth Century"
"The Vision of John Bunyan"

C.S. LEWIS ON LITERATURE

"Addison"
"A Note on Jane Austen"
"Shelley, Dryden, and Mr Eliot"
"Sir Walter Scott"
"William Morris"
"Kipling's World"
"High and Low Brows"

God in the Dock (1970)
"Myth Became Fact"
"On the Reading of Old Books"
"Meditation in a Toolshed"
"Bulverism"

C. S. Lewis on Stories and Other Essays on Literature (1982)
"On Stories"
"The Novels of Charles Williams"
"On Three Ways of Writing for Children"
"Sometimes Fairy Stories May Say Best What's to be Said"
"On Juvenile Tastes"
"The Hobbit"
"Tolkien's *The Lord of the Rings*"
"A Panegyric for Dorothy L Sayers"
"The Mythopoeic Gift of Rider Haggard"
"George Orwell"

ACKNOWLEDGEMENTS

My thanks to all those who have read all or part of the various incarnations of this book in its draft form. I am especially grateful to Michael Cavaghan-Pack for his wisdom and his detailed reading of one version of the entire script. My thanks also to Professor John Feehally, Professor James Como, Dr. Andrew Marfleet, the Revd Nick Benson, Will Vaus, and Richard Scott for their advice and suggestions. Special thanks also go to David Llewellyn Dodds for his expertise in a variety of critical areas, not least the literary-critical aspect of Lewis's letters.

To Robert Trexler, Editor at Winged Lion Press, I am especially indebted for his knowledge, enthusiasm, perseverance, encouragement, and the opportunity to bring this book to fruition.

Mystical Perelandra

My Lifelong Reading
of C. S. Lewis
& His Favorite Book

James Como

OTHER BOOKS FROM WINGED LION PRESS

C.S. LEWIS

No Ordinary People:
Twenty-one Friendships of C.S. Lewis
Joel Heck

The creator of the internet database Chronologically Lewis explores 21 friendships, some close and others casual, providing a look into the private life of one of the twentieth century's most engaging and effective writers. The book title comes from his famous sermon "The Weight of Glory".

The Leadership of C. S. Lewis:
Ten Traits to Encourage Change & Growth
Crystal Hurd

This book is for readers interested in developing leadership traits by examining how C. S. Lewis became such an influential spiritual leader for our times. The chapters include: Humility, Morality, Vision, Courage, Intellect, Compassion, Duty, Inspiration, Resilience, and Creativity.

C. S. Lewis: Views From Wake Forest:
Essays on C. S. Lewis
Michael Travers, editor

Contains sixteen scholarly presentations from the international C. S. Lewis convention in Wake Forest, NC. Walter Hooper shares his important essay "Editing C. S. Lewis," a chronicle of publishing decisions after Lewis' death in 1963.

> "Scholars from a variety of disciplines address a wide range of issues. The happy result is a fresh and expansive view of an author who well deserves this kind of thoughtful attention."
> Diana Pavlac Glyer, author of *The Company They Keep*

The Hidden Story of Narnia:
A Book-By-Book Guide to Lewis' Spiritual Themes
Will Vaus   (also available as an audiobook)

A book of insightful commentary equally suited for teens or adults – Will Vaus points out connections between the *Narnia* books and spiritual/biblical themes, as well as between ideas in the *Narnia* books and C. S. Lewis' other books. Learn what Lewis himself said about the overarching and unifying thematic structure of the Narnia books. That is what this book explores: what C. S. Lewis called "the hidden story" of Narnia. Each chapter includes questions for individual use or small group discussion.

Why I Believe in Narnia:
33 Reviews and Essays on the Life and Work of C. S. Lewis
James Como

Chapters range from reviews of critical books, documentaries and movies to evaluations of Lewis' books to biographical analysis.

> "A valuable, wide-ranging collection of essays by one of the best informed and most accute commentators on Lewis' work and ideas."
> Peter Schakel, author of *Imagination & the Arts in C. S. Lewis*

C. S. Lewis: His Literary Achievement
Colin Manlove

> "This is a positively brilliant book, written with splendor, elegance, profundity and evidencing an enormous amount of learning. This is probably not a book to give a first-time reader of Lewis. But for those who are more broadly read in the Lewis corpus this book is an absolute gold mine of information. The author gives us a magnificent overview of Lewis' many writings, tracing for us thoughts and ideas which recur throughout, and at the same time telling us how each book differs from the others. I think it is not extravagant to call C. S. Lewis: His Literary Achievement a tour de force."
> Robert Merchant, *St. Austin Review*, Book Review Editor

Speaking of Jack: A C. S. Lewis Discussion Guide
Will Vaus

Included here are introductions to most of Lewis' books as well as questions designed to stimulate discussion about Lewis' life and work. These materials have been "road-tested" with real groups made up of young and old, some very familiar with Lewis and some newcomers. *Speaking of Jack* may be used in an existing book discussion group, to start a C. S. Lewis Society, or as a guide to your own exploration of Lewis' books.

Light: C. S. Lewis' First and Final Short Story
Charlie W. Starr
Foreword by Walter Hooper

Charlie Starr explores the questions surrounding the "Light" manuscript, a later version of story titled "A Man Born Blind." The insights into this story provide a new key to understanding some of Lewis' most profound ideas.

> *"As literary journalism, both investigative and critical, it is top shelf"*
> James Como, author of *Remembering C. S. Lewis*

> *"Starr shines a new and illuninating light on one of Lewis' most intriguing stories"*
> Michael Ward, author of *Planet Narnia*

C. S. Lewis & Philosophy as a Way of Life:
His Philosophical Thoughts
Adam Barkman

C. S. Lewis is rarely thought of as a "philosopher" per se despite having both studied and taught philosophy for several years at Oxford. Lewis' long journey to Christianity was essentially philosophical – passing through seven different stages. This 624 page book is an invaluable reference for C. S. Lewis scholars and fans alike

C. S. Lewis' Top Ten: Influential Books and Authors, Volume One
Will Vaus

Based on his books, marginal notes, and personal letters, Will Vaus explores Lewis' reading of the ten books he said shaped his vocational attitude and philosophy of life. Volume One covers the first three authors/books: George MacDonald: *Phantastes*, G.K. Chesterton: *The Everlasting Man*, and Virgil: *The Aeneid*. Vaus offers a brief biography of each author with a helpful summary of their books.

> *"Thorough, comprehensive, and illuminating"*
> Rolland Hein, Author of *George MacDonald: Victorian Mythmaker*

C. S. Lewis' Top Ten: Influential Books and Authors, Volume Two
Will Vaus

Volume Two covers the following authors/books: George Herbert: *The Temple*, William Wordsworth: *The Prelude*, Rudopf Otto, *The Idea of the Holy*.

C. S. Lewis' Top Ten: Influential Books and Authors, Volume Three
Will Vaus

Volume Three covers the following authors/books: Boethius: *The Consolation of Philosophy*, James Boswell, *The Life of Samuel Johnson*, Charles Williams: *Descent into Hell*, A.J. Balfour: *Thiesm and Humanism*.

C. S. Lewis Goes to Heaven:
A Reader's Guide to The Great Divorce
David G. Clark

This is the first book devoted solely to this often neglected book and the first to reveal several important secrets Lewis concealed within the story. Lewis felt his imaginary trip to Hell and Heaven was far better than his book *The Screwtape Letters*, which has become a classic. Readers will discover the many literary and biblical influences Lewis utilized in writing his brilliant novel.

Joy and Poetic Imagination: Understanding C. S. Lewis' "Great War" with Owen Barfield and its Significance for Lewis' Conversion and Writings
Stephen Thorson

Author Stephen Thorson began writing this book over 30 years ago and published parts of it in articles during Barfield's lifetime. Barfield wrote to Thorson in 1983 saying, ""*...you have surveyed the divergence between Lewis and myself very fairly, and truly 'in depth...*'". This book explains the "Great War" between these two friends.

Mythopoeic Narnia: Memory, Metaphor, and Metamorphoses in C. S. Lewis' The Chronicles of Narnia
Salwa Khoddam

Dr. Khoddam offers a fresh approach to the *Narnia* books based on an inquiry into Lewis' readings and use of classical and Christian symbols. She explores the literary and intellectual contexts of these stories, the traditional myths and motifs, and places them in the company of the greatest Christian mythopoeic works of Western Literature.

Exploring the Eternal Goodness: Selected Writings of David L. Neuhouser
Joe Ricke and Lisa Ritchie, Editors

In 1997, due to David's perseverance, the Brown Collection of books by and about C. S. Lewis and related authors came to Taylor University and the Lewis and Friends Colloquium began. This book of selected writings reflects his scholarship in math and literature, as well as his musings on beauty and the imagination. The twenty-one tributes are an indication of the many lives he has influenced. This book is meant to acknowledge David L. Neuhouser for his contributions to scholarship and to honor his life of friendship, encouragement, and genuine goodness.

Inklings Forever, Volume X: Proceedings from the 10th Francis White Ewbank Colloquiunm on C. S. Lewis & Friends
Joe Ricke and Rick Hill, Editors

In June 2016, the 10th biennial Frances Ewbank Colloquium on C. S. Lewis and Friends convened at Taylor University with the special theme of "friendship." Many of the essays and creative pieces collected in this book explore the important relationships of Inklings-related authors, as well as the relationships between those authors and other, sometimes rather surprising, "friends." The year 2016 marked the 90th anniversary of the first meeting of C. S. Lewis and J.R.R. Tolkien – a creative friendship of epic proportions

> What a feast! It is rare that a book of proceedings captures the energy and spirit of the conference itself: this one does. I recommend it.
> Diana Pavlac Glyer, Professor of English at Azusa Pacific University and author of *The Company They Keep* and *Bandersnatch: C. S. Lewis, J. R. R. Tolkien, and the Creative Collaboration of the Inklings*

The Faithful Imagination: Papers from the 2018 Francis White Ewbank Colloquiunm on C. S. Lewis & Friends
Joe Ricke and Ashley Chu, Editors

> *We live in a world that desperately needs more of the Inklings' wit, wisdoe, and winsomeness. The Faithful Imagination contains something for everyone and represents one of the few places where such things can be found..*
> Devin Brown, Professor of English at Asbury University and author of *A Life Observed: A Spiritual Biography of C.S. Lewis.*

Sunbeams and Bottles:
The Theology, Thought, and Reading of C.S. Lewis
James Prothero

C.S. Lewis once said of Christ that he was the most elusive of teachers and that trying to systematize the Lord's teaching was like trying to bottle sunbeams. Sunbeams and Bottles is not only a response to attempts in the last decade to tie Lewis to particular political and social agendas, but it is also a fresh look at his thought in light of his reading. The author posits that Lewis really was a theologian in spite of his protests against the idea.

C. S. Lewis Goes to Hell
A Companion and Study Guide to The Screwtape Letters
William O'Flaherty

The creator and host of "All About Jack" has written a guide to *The Screwtape Letters* suitable for groups or individuals, featuring an index of themes, summaries of each letter, questions for reflection, and over a half-dozen appendices of useful information.

In the Footsteps of C. S. Lewis:
A Photographic Pilgrimage to the British Isles
Will Vaus

Over the course of thirty years, Will Vaus has journeyed to the British Isles many times to walk in the footsteps of C. S. Lewis. His private photographs of the significant places in Lewis' life have captured the imagination of audiences in the US and UK to whom he has lectured on the Oxford don and his work. This, in turn, prompted the idea of this collection of 78 full-color photographs, interwoven with details about Lewis' life and work. The combination of words and pictures make this a wonderful addition to the library of all Lewis scholars and readers.

Mystical Perelandra:
My Lifelong Reading of CS Lewis and His Favorite Book
James Como

> "Como draws us into the mysterious heart of the reader's experience, living within rather than merely analyzing Lewis' literary vision. Como's reflections on Perelandra transport us, like Ransom, to a world of myth and meaning much greater than a book."
>
> Brenton Dickieson,
> Author of the popular blog APilgrimInNarnia.com and Lecturer of Literature at several universities

CHRISTIAN LIVING

Keys to Growth: Meditations on the Acts of the Apostles
Will Vaus

Every living thing or person requires certain ingredients in order to grow, and if a thing or person is not growing, it is dying. *The Acts of the Apostles* is a book that is all about growth. Will Vaus has been meditating and preaching on *Acts* for the past 30 years. In this volume, he offers the reader forty-one keys from the entire book of Acts to unlock spiritual growth in everyday life.

Open Before Christmas: Devotional Thoughts For The Holiday Season
Will Vaus

Author Will Vaus seeks to deepen the reader's knowledge of Advent and Christmas leading up to Epiphany. Readers are provided with devotional thoughts for each day that help them to experience this part of the Church Year perhaps in a more spiritually enriching way than ever before.

God's Love Letter: Reflections on I John
Will Vaus

Various words for "love" appear thirty-five times in the five brief chapters of I John. This book invites you on a journey of reading and reflection: reading this book in the New Testament and reflecting on God's love for us, our love for God, and our love for one another.

Jogging with G.K. Chsterton: 65 Earthshaking Expeditions
Robert Moore-Jumonville

Jogging with G.K. Chesterton is a showcase for the merry mind of Chesterton. But Chesterton's lighthearted wit always runs side-by-side with his weighty wisdom. These 65 "earthshaking expeditions" will keep you smiling and thinking from start to finish. You'll be entertained, challenged, and spiritually uplifted as you take time to breathe in the fresh morning air and contemplate the wonders of the world.

> "This is a delightfully improbable book in which Chesterton puts us through our spiritual and intellectual exercises."
> Joseph Pearce, author of *Wisdom and Innocence: A Life of G.K. Chesterton*

GEORGE MACDONALD

Phantastes by George MacDonald: Annotated Edition
John Pennington and Roderick McGillis, Editors

Phantastes was a groundbreaking book in 1858 and continues to be a seminal example of great fantasy literature. Its elusive meaning is both alluring and perplexing, inviting readers to experience a range of deep feelings and a sense of profound truth. This annotated edition, by two renowned MacDonald scholars, provides a wealth of information to better understand and enjoy this masterpiece.

Crossing a Great Frontier: Essays on George MacDonald's Phantastes
John Pennington, Editor

> "This is the first collection of scholarly essays on George MacDonald's seminal romance Phantastes. Appropriately to the age of its hero Anodos, here we have twenty-one of the best essays written on Phantastes from 1972 onwards, in which straightforward literary analysis works together with contextual, psychological, metaphysical, alchemical and scientific approaches to the elucidation of this moving and elusive work."
> Colin Manlove, author of *Scotland's Forgotten Treasure: The Visionary Novels of George MacDonald*

Lilith by George MacDonald: Annotated Scholarly Edition
John Pennington & Roderick McGillis, Editors
Following the acclaim of their scholarly edition of MacDonald's *Phantastes*, these editors combine their expertise to create a foundational resource to enjoy *Lilith*, a masterpiece of fantasy literature. Over 500 footnotes, seven appendices, reviews, and more. [forthcoming publication]

Behind the Back of the North Wind:
Essays on George MacDonald's Classic Book
Edited and with Introduction by John Pennington and Roderick McGillis

The unique blend of fairy tale atmosphere and social realism in this novel laid the groundwork for modern fantasy literature. Sixteen essays by various authors are accompanied by an instructive introduction, extensive index, and beautiful illustrations.

Diary of an Old Soul & The White Page Poems
George MacDonald and Betty Aberlin

The first edition of George MacDonald's book of daily poems included a blank page opposite each page of poems. Readers were invited to write their own reflections on the "white page." Betty Aberlin responded to MacDonald's invitation with daily poems of her own.

> *Betty Aberlin's close readings of George MacDonald's verses and her thoughtful responses to them speak clearly of her poetic gifts and spiritual intelligence.*
> Luci Shaw, poet

George MacDonald: Literary Heritage and Heirs
Roderick McGillis, editor

This latest collection of 14 essays sets a new standard that will influence MacDonald studies for many more years. George MacDonald experts are increasingly evaluating his entire corpus within the nineteenth century context.

> *This comprehensive collection represents the best of contemporary scholarship on George MacDonald.*
> Rolland Hein, author of *George MacDonald: Victorian Mythmaker*

In the Near Loss of Everything: George MacDonald's Son in America
Dale Wayne Slusser

In the summer of 1887, George MacDonald's son Ronald, newly engaged to artist Louise Blandy, sailed from England to America to teach school. The next summer he returned to England to marry Louise and bring her back to America. On August 27, 1890, Louise died leaving him with an infant daughter. Ronald once described losing a beloved spouse as "the near loss of everything". Dale Wayne Slusser unfolds this poignant story with unpublished letters and photos that give readers a glimpse into the close-knit MacDonald family. Also included is Ronald's essay about his father, *George MacDonald: A Personal Note*, plus a selection from Ronald's 1922 fable, *The Laughing Elf*, about the necessity of both sorrow and joy in life.

A Novel Pulpit: Sermons From George MacDonald's Fiction
David L. Neuhouser

Each of the sermons has an introduction giving some explanation of the setting of the sermon or of the plot. *"MacDonald's novels are both stimulating and thought-provoking. This collection of sermons from ten novels serve to bring out the 'freshness and brilliance' of MacDonald's message." from the author's introduction*

Through the Year with George MacDonald: 366 Daily Readings
Rolland Hein, editor

These page-length excerpts from sermons, novels and letters are given an appropriate theme/heading and a complementary Scripture passage for daily reading. An inspiring introduction to the artistic soul and Christian vision of George MacDonald.

Shadows and Chivalry:
C. S. Lewis and George MacDonald on Suffering, Evil, and Death
Jeff McInnis

Shadows and Chivalry studies the influence of George MacDonald upon one of the most influential writers of modern times, C. S. Lewis—the creator of Narnia, literary critic, and best-selling apologist. Without ever ceasing to be a story of one man's influence upon another, the study also serves as an exploration of each writer's thought on, and literary visions of, good and evil.

The Downstretched Hand:
Individual Development in MacDonald's Major Fantasies for Children
Lesley Willis Smith

Smith demonstrates that MacDonald is fully aware of the need to integrate the unconscious into the conscious in order to achieve mature individuation. However, for MacDonald, true maturity and fulfillment can only be gained through a relationship with God. By exploring MacDonald's major biblical themes into his own myth, Smith reveals his literary genius and profound understanding of the human psyche. Smith interacts with other leading scholarship and in the context of other works by MacDonald, especially those written during the same time period.

Biography & Memoirs

Sheldon Vanauken:
The Man Who Received "A Severe Mercy"
Will Vaus

In this biography we discover: Vanauken the struggling student, the bon-vivant lover, the sailor who witnessed the bombing of Pearl Harbor, the seeker who returned to faith through C. S. Lewis, the beloved professor of English literature and history, the feminist and anti-war activist who participated in the March on the Pentagon, the bestselling author, and Vanauken the convert to Catholicism. What emerges is the portrait of a man relentlessly in search of beauty, love, and truth, a man who believed that, in the end, he found all three.

> *"This is a charming biography about a doubly charming man who wrote a triply charming book. It is a great way to meet the man behind A Severe Mercy."*
> Peter Kreeft, author of *Jacob's Ladder: 10 Steps to Truth*

Remembering Roy Campbell:
The Memoirs of his Daughters, Anna and Tess
Introduction by Judith Lütge Coullie, Editor
Preface by Joseph Pearce

Anna and Teresa Campbell were the daughters of the handsome young South African poet and writer, Roy Campbell (1901-1957), and his beautiful English wife, Mary Garman. In their frank and moving memoirs, Anna and Tess recall the extraordinary, and often very difficult, lives they shared with their exceptional parents. Over 50 photos, 344 footnotes, timeline of Campbell's life, and complete index.

My Journey with C.S. Lewis and Other Companions
Will Vaus

This is the story of a spiritual journey with C. S. Lewis and other literary companions, a memoir of a lifetime of reading. Lewis enthusiasts will particularly enjoy descriptions of many visits to Lewis landmarks in the British Isles and the year Vaus and his family spent in Ireland with Merrie and Douglas Gresham (Lewis' stepson).

www.ingramcontent.com/pod-product-compliance
Lightning Source LLC
Chambersburg PA
CBHW060522080526
44586CB00012B/576